A Comprehensive Study of SQL

A Comprehensive Study of SQL: Practice and Implementation is designed as a textbook and provides a comprehensive approach to SQL (Structured Query Language), the standard programming language for defining, organizing, and exploring data in relational databases. It demonstrates how to leverage the two most vital tools for data query and analysis– SQL and Excel – to perform comprehensive data analysis without the need for a sophisticated and expensive data mining tool or application.

Features

- Provides a complete collection of modeling techniques, beginning with fundamentals and gradually progressing through increasingly complex real-world case studies.
- Explains how to build, populate, and administer high-performance databases and develop robust SQL-based applications.
- Gives a solid foundation in best practices and relational theory.
- Offers self-contained lessons on key SQL concepts or techniques at the end of each chapter using numerous illustrations and annotated examples.

This book is aimed primarily at advanced undergraduates and graduates with a background in computer science and information technology. Researchers and professionals will also find this book useful.

A Comprehensive Study of SQL
Practice and Implementation

Jagdish Chandra Patni

CRC Press
Taylor & Francis Group
Boca Raton London New York

CRC Press is an imprint of the
Taylor & Francis Group, an **informa** business

A CHAPMAN & HALL BOOK

First edition published 2023
by CRC Press
6000 Broken Sound Parkway NW, Suite 300, Boca Raton, FL 33487-2742

and by CRC Press
4 Park Square, Milton Park, Abingdon, Oxon, OX14 4RN

CRC Press is an imprint of Taylor & Francis Group, LLC

Library of Congress Cataloging-in-Publication Data
Names: Patni, Jagdish Chandra, author.
Title: A comprehensive study of SQL : practice and implementation / Jagdish Chandra Patni.
Description: First edition. | Boca Raton : Chapman & Hall/CRC Press, 2023. | Includes bibliographical references and index. |
Identifiers: LCCN 2022026700 (print) | LCCN 2022026701 (ebook) | ISBN 9781032348407 (hardback) | ISBN 9781032349756 (paperback) | ISBN 9781003324690 (ebook)
Subjects: LCSH: Microsoft Excel (Computer file)--Textbooks. | SQL (Computer program language)--Textbooks. | Relational databases--Textbooks. | Querying (Computer science)--Textbooks.
Classification: LCC QA76.73.S67 P3775 2023 (print) | LCC QA76.73.S67 (ebook) | DDC 005.54--dc23/eng/20220920
LC record available at https://lccn.loc.gov/2022026700

ISBN: 978-1-032-34840-7 (hbk)
ISBN: 978-1-032-34975-6 (pbk)
ISBN: 978-1-003-32469-0 (ebk)

DOI: 10.1201/9781003324690

Typeset in Palatino
by SPi Technologies India Pvt Ltd (Straive)

This book "*A Comprehensive Study of SQL: Practice and Implementation*" is dedicated to my beloved parents Late Sh. Prayag Datt Patni and Smt. Haripriya Patni; I am here in this beautiful world just because of your blessings and guidance. My father, now you are not with us, but I know you are still giving your continuous blessings to all.

My wife, Priyanka Patni always motivates me to do new things, she always reminds me that you can do wonders if you try for the same, so this book is the result of this continuous motivation.

I dedicate this book to my loving kids, Shrey and Parisha, who gave me strength and love during the journey of this book; I took their time while working day and night.

Last but not least, I dedicate this book to all my family members, gurus, colleagues, friends, and my beloved students for motivating and continuous support for this wonderful purpose.

Dr. Jagdish Chandra Patni
Jain University Bangalore

Contents

Preface.. xiii
Biography xv
Acknowledgement... xvii

1. **Database Systems** 1
    1.1   Introduction to Databases.. 1
        1.1.1   Difference between a Database and a Spreadsheet?.................. 2
        1.1.2   Database Challenges.. 2
        1.1.3   Advantages of DBMS 3
        1.1.4   Disadvantages of DBMS 3
        1.1.5   Types of Databases.. 4
                1.1.5.1   Relational Databases 4
                1.1.5.2   Object-Oriented Databases 4
                1.1.5.3   Distributed Databases... 4
                1.1.5.4   Data Warehouses 4
                1.1.5.5   NoSQL Databases... 4
                1.1.5.6   Graph Databases 4
                1.1.5.7   On-Line Transaction Processing Databases............ 4
                1.1.5.8   Open-Source Databases... 5
                1.1.5.9   Cloud Databases.. 5
                1.1.5.10 Multimodel Database 5
                1.1.5.11 Document/JSON Database.. 5
                1.1.5.12 Self-Driving Databases 5
    1.2   Database Models 5
        1.2.1   Hierarchical Databases.. 6
        1.2.2   Network Databases.. 7
        1.2.3   Object-Oriented Model 7
        1.2.4   Graph Databases Model.. 8
        1.2.5   Entity–Relationship Model... 8
        1.2.6   Document Databases Model 9
        1.2.7   NoSQL Databases Model... 10
        1.2.8   The Relational Model 10
        1.2.9   Terminology.. 12
    1.3   Database Languages 15
        1.3.1   Data Definition Language (DDL) 15
        1.3.2   Data Manipulation Language (DML) 15
        1.3.3   Data Control Language (DCL) 16
        1.3.4   Data Retrieval Language (DRL)... 16
    1.4   SQL: A Nonprocedural Language 17
        1.4.1   MySQL.. 17
        1.4.2   SQL Examples.. 19

1.5	Data Types in SQL	20
1.6	Creating Database	22
1.7	Use of MySQL	22
1.8	Summary	25
	References	25

2. Creating and Manipulating Database 27
2.1	Data Definition Language (DDL)	27
	2.1.1 Create Command	27
	2.1.2 ALTER Command	28
	2.1.3 DROP Command	29
	2.1.4 TRUNCATE Command	30
	2.1.5 Rename Command	30
2.2	Data Manipulation Language (DML)	31
	2.2.1 INSERT INTO Command	31
	2.2.2 DELETE Command	31
	2.2.3 Update Command	32
	2.2.4 SELECT Command	33
2.3	Data Control Language (DCL)	34
2.4	Transaction Control Language (TCL)	35
2.5	Database Structure	36
2.6	Examples	38
2.7	Summary	43
	References	43

3. Data and Integrity Constraints 45
3.1	Introduction	45
	3.1.1 Domain Integrity	45
	3.1.2 Entity Integrity	46
	3.1.3 Referential Integrity	47
	3.1.4 User-Defined Integrity	47
3.2	Types of Keys in DBMS	48
	3.2.1 Super Key	48
	3.2.2 Candidate Key	48
	3.2.3 Primary Key	49
	3.2.4 Alternate Key	51
	3.2.5 Foreign Key	51
3.3	Check Constraints	53
3.4	Unique Constraints	54
3.5	Domain Constraints	55
3.6	Summary	56
	References	56

4. Query Execution and Aggregate Functions 59
4.1	Select Statement	59
	4.1.1 Single Attribute Selection	59
	4.1.2 Multiple Attribute Selection	60
	4.1.3 Complete Table Selection	61
	4.1.4 Distinct Selection	62

	4.1.5	Where Clause	63
4.2	Aggregate Functions		64
	4.2.1	Average	64
	4.2.2	Count()	66
	4.2.3	Sum()	67
	4.2.4	Min()	67
	4.2.5	Max()	68
4.3	Order By Clause		68
4.4	Group By Clause		71
4.5	Having Clause		72
4.6	Examples		73
4.7	Summary		74
References			75

5. SQL Server vs. Oracle 77
5.1	Design Schema		77
	5.1.1	Similarities between SQL Server and Oracle	78
	5.1.2	Schema Object Names	78
	5.1.3	Design Issues	78
		5.1.3.1 Data Types	79
		5.1.3.2 Entity Integrity Constraints	81
		5.1.3.3 Referential Integrity Constraints	81
		5.1.3.4 Unique Key Constraints	82
		5.1.3.5 Check Constraints	82
5.2	Data Types		82
5.3	Data Storage		84
5.4	DML Statement from SQL Server vs. Oracle		84
	5.4.1	Connecting to the Database	86
	5.4.2	SELECT Statement	86
5.5	Microsoft SQL Server vs. Oracle: The Same but Different		87
5.6	Summary		88
References			88

6. Conditional Statements and Operators in SQL 89
6.1	Introduction		89
6.2	Conditional Evaluation		89
6.3	Types of Condition		90
	6.3.1	IF Condition	90
	6.3.2	The CASE Statement	90
	6.3.3	While Statement	91
	6.3.4	For Statement	92
6.4	Operators		94
	6.4.1	Arithmetic Operators	95
	6.4.2	Comparison Operator	100
	6.4.3	Logical Operators	104
		6.4.3.1 ANY Operator	104
		6.4.3.2 ALL Operator	105
		6.4.3.3 AND Operator	106
		6.4.3.4 OR Operator	106

6.4.3.5   Between Operator 107
6.4.3.6   EXISTS Operator.. 108
6.4.3.7   IN Operator 108
6.4.3.8   LIKE Operator 108
6.4.3.9   NOT Operator.. 110
6.4.3.10   IS NULL Operator 111
6.4.3.11   UNIQUE Operator 112
6.5   Summary 113
References 113

7. **Nested Query and Join** 115
7.1   Understanding Subquery.. 115
7.2   Understanding Nested Query... 117
7.3   Join Operator 118
7.3.1   INNER JOIN 119
7.3.2   SELF JOIN 121
7.3.3   OUTER JOIN 122
7.3.3.1   Left OUTER JOIN.. 122
7.3.3.2   Right OUTER JOIN 124
7.3.3.3   Full OUTER JOIN.. 125
7.4   Summary 126
References 126

8. **Views, Indexes, and Sequence** 129
8.1   Introduction to VIEW 129
8.2   Types of Views.. 130
8.2.1   Simple View 130
8.2.2   Composite View 133
8.3   Indexes... 135
8.4   Types of Index... 136
8.4.1   Simple Index 136
8.4.2   Composite Index 136
8.4.3   Unique Index 137
8.4.4   Reverse Index 137
8.4.5   Function-Based Index.. 138
8.5   Sequences 139
8.6   Types of Sequences 139
8.6.1   Auto-Increment Sequence 139
8.6.2   Cycle Sequence.. 140
8.6.3   No Cycle Sequence 141
8.7   Examples 141
8.8   Summary 143
References 143

9. **PL/SQL**... 145
9.1   Introduction to PL/SQL.. 145
9.2   Features of PL/SQL 145
9.3   Advantages of PL/SQL.. 146

9.4 Data Types in PL/SQL 146
9.5 Variables and Constants 147
9.6 PL/SQL Literals 148
9.7 Examples 149
  9.7.1 IF Statement 149
    9.7.1.1 IF-THEN Statement 149
    9.7.1.2 IF-THEN-ELSE Statement 149
  9.7.2 Case Statement 150
  9.7.3 Loop Statement 151
  9.7.4 Continue Statement 156
  9.7.5 GOTO Statement 157
9.8 Summary 158
References 159

10. **Procedures and Functions** 161
10.1 Understanding Functions 161
10.2 Features and Advantages 161
10.3 Types of Functions 162
10.4 Return Types 165
10.5 Procedures 166
10.6 Difference between Function and Procedure 167
10.7 Examples 167
10.8 Summary 169
References 170

11. **Cursors and Triggers** 171
11.1 Understanding Cursor 171
11.2 Types of Cursors 171
  11.2.1 Implicit Cursors 171
  11.2.2 Explicit Cursors 173
11.3 Examples of Cursors 174
11.4 Uses of Cursors 175
11.5 Understanding Trigger 175
11.6 Types of Triggers 176
  11.6.1 Row-Level Trigger 176
  11.6.2 Table-Level Triggers 177
  11.6.3 After Trigger 177
  11.6.4 Before Trigger 178
11.7 Trigger Example 178
11.8 Summary 181
References 181

12. **Database Change Management** 183
12.1 Overview 183
12.2 Database Definitions 185
  12.2.1 Scope Specification 185
  12.2.2 Versions 186
  12.2.3 Exporting/Importing Dictionaries 186

12.3 Comparisons 187
    12.3.1 Defining Dictionary Comparisons 188
    12.3.2 Dictionary Comparison Sources 188
12.4 Synchronizations 188
    12.4.1 Defining Dictionary Synchronizations 189
        12.4.1.1 Source and Destination 189
        12.4.1.2 Synchronization Mode 189
    12.4.2 Creating Synchronization Versions 189
12.5 Summary 190
References 190

13. Sample Questions and Answers 191
13.1 Company Database Example 191
13.2 Fill in the Blanks 202
13.3 True and False 203
13.4 Multiple Choice Questions 203

Index 215

Preface

Managing data is a critical task when it comes to a scale, and we need a powerful management tool or program to handle this huge amount of data. These specialized sets of programs are known as database management system, and SQL is one of the powerful tools for managing the data.

SQL stands for a structured query language used to manage the relational database management system where we store the data in the form of rows and columns. SQL has different sets of languages for defining the databases, managing the databases, retrieving the databases, and controlling the user access in the database. This book focuses on the basics of SQL, starting from creating the databases, manipulating the databases, constraints that make our database stronger, concepts of programming languages, functions, and procedures, as well as advanced concepts of triggers and cursors. This book also covers the difference between SQL and Oracle with similarities and differences. This book also covers the basics of change management in the database system.

This book comes with the proper syntax of each one of the topics with practical examples with proper explained output. This book contains real-life examples for a better understanding of the topics with proper explanation.

This book guarantees to bridge the gap between theoretical knowledge and practical implementations with the proper understanding of concepts. We would like to invite suggestions from our readers to improve the content of this book.

This book is divided into 13 chapters, and each chapter is connected with other chapters. The chapter-wise details are as follows.

Chapter 1: This chapter gives the basics of the databases in terms of practical implementation with features, advantages, and disadvantages.

Chapter 2: This chapter gives detailed descriptions of defining, manipulating, retrieving, and controlling the database with proper syntax and examples.

Chapter 3: This chapter describes the various types of database constraints that make our database stronger and safer. This chapter also discussed the various types of keys used in the databases and their practical implementation.

Chapter 4: This chapter shows the effective and efficient retrieval of records from the databases with different types of select statements. Also discussed are the different types of aggregate functions.

Chapter 5: In this chapter, the concepts SQL and Oracle are discussed with similarities and differences between them.

Chapter 6: This chapter discusses conditional statements and different types of operators used in SQL.

Chapter 7: This chapter explains the concepts of subqueries and joins and how we can use them and vice-versa.

Chapter 8: Here, we discuss the concepts of views, indexes sequences, and how these topics are used in the database.

Chapter 9: This chapter explains the basics of programming logic in SQL with proper syntax and examples for each one of the programming logic used in SQL.

Chapter 10: Here, we have introduced the concept of functions and procedures in SQL and the difference between the functions and procedures.

Chapter 11: This chapter discusses the advanced concepts of triggers and cursors.

Chapter 12: Change management is important when we want to switch the database from one to another. This chapter focuses on all the basics of change management.

Chapter 13: A number of examples and questions related to the topics discussed in previous chapters are given.

Finally, this book aims to provide real implementation issues and possible solutions to the readers. As most of readers do not know about the programming logics in database, this book will give them a glimpse of programming logics with the concepts of functions, procedures, cursors, triggers, etc. This book is suitable for all readers, from beginners to expert.

Biography

 **Dr. Jagdish Chandra Patni** is working as a Professor at Faculty of Engineering and Technology, Jain University Bangalore, India. He did his Ph.D. in the area of High Performance computing in 2016. He completed his M. Tech. and B. Tech. in 2009 and 2004, respectively. Dr Patni is actively working in the research areas of Database Systems, High Performance computing, Software Engineering, Machine Learning, and IoT. He has authored more than 50 research articles in the journal and conferences of repute nationally and internationally. Dr Patni has authored 5 plus books and book chapters with international publishers like Springer. He is an active Guest Editor/Reviewer of various referred International journals. He has delivered 15 Keynote/Guest speeches in India and abroad. He has organized multiple conferences/seminars/workshops/FDPs in India and abroad. He has been awarded by researcher Excellence award in 2021 by the Government of Uttarakhand & UCOST, Young Scientist Award 2021 by UCOST Dehradun and Divya Himgiri, Teacher of the year 2020 by Govt. of Uttarakhand, best paper award by Hosei University Tokyo, Japan in 2020, and many more. He is a Senior member of IEEE, Member ACM, MIE, IEANG, IACSIT, Vigyan Bharti, etc.

Acknowledgement

I shall ever remain thankfully indebted to all those learned souls, my present and former teachers, known and unknown hands who directly or indirectly motivated me to achieve my goal and enlightened me with the touch of their knowledge and constant encouragement. This is an extremely significant and joyous opportunity bestowed upon me by God, to think about and thank all those persons.

First and foremost, I wish to express my love to Students Bhavy Kharbanda and Aryan Anand Singh, School of Computer Science, University of Petroleum and Energy Studies, Dehradun, for their support in preparing the content of this book.

I am very much thankful for the management, colleagues, and staff of the University of Petroleum and Energy Studies Dehradun, who give me such a wonderful environment and time to do good things and always motivated me for research.

I would sincerely thank Dr. Amit Agarwal, Director, APJ Abdul Kalam Institute of Technology, Tanakpur Champawat, Uttarakhand, for helpful discussions, advice, motivation, and showing trust on me.

I am grateful to my mentor, guru Dr. Mahendra Singh Aswal, Gurukula Kangri University Haridwar, for reviewing my work, and more importantly, for teaching me how to improve the content and always support for a good cause.

I am very much thankful to Dr. Sunil Rai, Vice Chancellor, UPES Dehradun, Dr. Ram Sharma, PVC, UPES Dehradun Dr. Neelu Jyothi Ahuja Cluster Head Systemics, and Dr. T P Singh Cluster Head Informatics, for their continuous support and motivation.

I would like to express my gratitude to Dr. Ravi Tomar, Dr. Tanupriya Choudhury, Dr. Ankur Dumka, and Dr. Hitesh Kumar Sharma, who took their time to review my work and give their positive comments to improve the work.

Finally, I am forever indebted to my parents, wife, and two lovely kids: Shrey Patni and Parisha Patni, and the rest of my family members. My wife, Priyanka Patni, has been a great source of inspiration to me. None of this would have been possible without her love, support, and continuous encouragement. My parents' blessings and prayers have always accompanied me. Their love keeps me working hard and hard.

1

Database Systems

A database is a well-defined collection of structured information, or data, which is typically stored digitally in a computer system. The control unit that usually controls the database is known as the database management system (DBMS). The data and the DBMS, along with the applications that are related to them, are referred to as a database system, often abbreviated as just a database. The database is a collection of interrelated data that is used to effortlessly retrieve, manipulate, insert and delete the data. It is also used to organize the data in the form of a table including rows and columns, schema, views, reports, etc.

The most common type of data within various databases in operation today is typically patterned in rows and columns in a series of tables to make processing and data manipulation efficient and easy. Further, this data can be easily organized, accessed, managed, modified, updated, and controlled. Most databases use structured query language (SQL) to write and manipulate the data. SQL is a programming language that is used by nearly all relational databases to manipulate, define data, query data, and provide access control.

A database typically requires an extensive database software program known as a DBMS. A DBMS serves as an interface between the database and its end users or programs that help the user retrieve, update, and manage how the information is organized and optimized. A DBMS also facilitates error control of databases, enabling various administrative operations, such as performance monitoring, tuning, and backup and recovery of the data.

Some examples of popular database software or DBMSs include MySQL, Microsoft SQL Server, Microsoft Access, Oracle Database, FileMaker Pro and dBASE.

1.1 Introduction to Databases

Databases have evolved dramatically since their beginning in the early 1960s. Navigational databases, such as the hierarchical database (which was in the form of a tree-like model and allowed only a one-to-many relationship) and the network database (a more flexible model that allowed multiple relationships), were the original models used to store and manipulate data. These early systems were simple to understand, but they were inflexible. In the 1980s, relational databases became popular, followed by another type of database that is object-oriented databases in the 1990s. Nowadays, NoSQL databases are in demand as the growth of the internet and the need for faster speed and processing of unstructured data have increased. Today, cloud and self-driving databases are setting up new records regarding how data is collected, stored, managed, manipulated, and utilized.

Database software is used to create, edit, manipulate, and maintain database files and documentation, enabling easier file creation, data entry, data editing, updating the files, and reporting. This software also handles data storage, backup and security, multi-access control, and reporting. Strong database security is especially important these days, as data theft has become more frequent everywhere. Database software is sometimes also referred to as a "DBMS."

Database software makes data management simpler by enabling users to store data in a structured form of rows and columns and then access it. It generally has a graphical interface to help create and manage the data, and in some cases, users can construct their databases as per their needs by using database software.

1.1.1 Difference between a Database and a Spreadsheet?

Databases and spreadsheets (such as Microsoft Excel) are both appropriate ways to store information. The major differences can be inferred by observing these factors:

- In what way is the data stored?
- Who can access the data?
- How much data can be stored?
- How can the data be manipulated?

Spreadsheets were originally designed for a single user, and their characteristics reflect that. They're great for one user or a small number of users who don't need to do a lot of complicated manipulations on the data. Databases, on the other hand, are designed in such a way that they can hold much larger collections of well-defined information—even massive amounts, sometimes. Database allows multiple users at the same time to quickly and securely access and manipulates the data using highly complex logic, algorithms, and queries.

1.1.2 Database Challenges

Today's large enterprise databases are constructed to support very complex queries and expected to deliver immediate responses to those queries. As a result, all the database administrators are frequently called upon to employ a wide variety of techniques to help improve performance. Some common challenges that they can face are:

- **Absorbing significant increases in data volume:** The overburden of data coming in from sensors, census, connected machines, and plenty of other sources keeps database administrators scrambling to manage and organize their organization's data efficiently.
- **Ensuring data security:** Hackers are getting more inventive these days, and data can be easily breached. It's more important than anything else to ensure that data is secure but also easily accessible to users without being muddled.
- **Keeping up with demand:** We are in the 21st century, and in today's fast-moving business environment, companies need real-time access to their data to cope with the competition in the market and take timely decisions and advantage of new opportunities.
- **Managing and maintaining the database and infrastructure:** Database administrators must continuously check on the problems associated with the database

and perform preventative maintenance, as well as apply software patches and upgrades. Whenever the databases become more complex and data volumes grow, organizations are faced with the expense of hiring additional manpower to monitor and take care of their databases.

- **Removing limits on scalability:** For a business to survive in such a competitive environment, it needs to grow and its data management must grow along with it. But it's very difficult for database administrators to predict how much capacity the organization will require, particularly with real-time databases.

- **Ensuring data occupancy, data authority, or latency requirements:** Some organizations have use cases that are more convenient to run on premises. In those cases, engineered systems and programs preconfigured and preoptimized for running the database are ideal for its working. Customers achieve higher availability of the data, better and improved performance, and up to 40% lower cost with Oracle Exadata.

1.1.3 Advantages of DBMS

- **Controls database redundancy:** Data redundancy occurs when the same piece of data is stored in more than one or two places. DBMS can control data redundancy as it stores all data in one single database file, and that recorded data is placed in the database.

- **Data sharing:** In DBMS, the authorized users of an organization can share the data among multiple users according to their needs.

- **Easy maintenance:** It can be easily maintained due to the centralized nature of the database system.

- **Reduce time:** It reduces the development time and maintenance need of the database.

- **Backup:** In case of any hardware or software failures, it can provide backup and recovery subsystems that create an automatic backup of data and restores the data if required.

- **Multiple user interfaces:** It provides different user interfaces, such as graphical user interfaces and application program interfaces simultaneously.

1.1.4 Disadvantages of DBMS

- **Cost of hardware and software:** It requires high-speed data processors and a huge memory size to run DBMS software.

- **Size:** It occupies large storage of disks and large memory to run them efficiently without any failure.

- **Complexity:** A database system creates additional complexity and requirements to coordinate everything together.

- **Higher impact of failure:** Failure can highly impact the database because, in most organizations, all the data is stored in a single database, and if the database is damaged due to electric failure or database corruption, then the important and valuable data may be lost forever.

1.1.5 Types of Databases

There exist many different types of databases. The best database for a specific organization depends on the needs of the organization and the work they intend to do using the database.

1.1.5.1 Relational Databases

Relational databases came into existence in the 1980s. Items in a relational database are organized as a set of tables using various rows and columns. Relational database technology provides the most systematic and flexible way to access structured information.

1.1.5.2 Object-Oriented Databases

Information in an object-oriented database is stored in the form of objects. It is similar to the representation that we did in object-oriented programming.

1.1.5.3 Distributed Databases

A distributed database consists of two or more files located in different areas. The database may be stored on multiple systems, either located in the same physical location or can be scattered over different networks.

1.1.5.4 Data Warehouses

A data warehouse is a central repository for data; it is a type of database specifically designed for instant query and analysis.

1.1.5.5 NoSQL Databases

A NoSQL, or nonrelational database, allows unstructured and semistructured data other than tables to be stored and manipulated (in contrast to a relational database, which explains how all data inserted into the database must be composed and should be well structured). NoSQL databases grew popular as the complexity in the data formats increased and web applications became more common.

1.1.5.6 Graph Databases

A graph database stores data in the form of a tree in terms of entities and the relationships between these entities.

1.1.5.7 On-Line Transaction Processing Databases

An OLTP database is a speedy, analytic database designed for huge and multiple numbers of transactions performed by multiple users.

Only a few of the several types of databases are in use today. Other, less common databases are customized to specific scientific, financial, or other functions. In addition to the different database types, changes in technology development approaches and dramatic advancements in technology, such as the cloud and automation, are boosting databases in entirely new directions.

1.1.5.8 Open-Source Databases

An open-source database system is the one whose source code is open source that is available for all; such databases could be SQL or NoSQL databases as per the requirements.

1.1.5.9 Cloud Databases

A cloud database is a collection of data, either structured or unstructured, that resides on a cloud computing platform owned by a private, public, or hybrid organization. There are two types of cloud database models: traditional database and database as a service (DBaaS). In the DBaaS database, administrative tasks and maintenance are performed by a service provider.

1.1.5.10 Multimodel Database

Multimodel databases combine different types of database models into a single, just like a metamodel, integrated back end. This means they can accommodate various data types in one single model.

1.1.5.11 Document/JSON Database

This database is designed for storing, retrieving, and managing document-oriented information; document databases are a modern way to store data in JSON format rather than using rows and columns.

1.1.5.12 Self-Driving Databases

The newest and the most recent groundbreaking type of database, self-driving databases (also known as autonomous databases), are cloud-based database and use machine learning to automate database maintenance, security, backups, updates, performance, and other routine management tasks that database administrators traditionally performed.

1.2 Database Models

There are several types of database models:

1. Hierarchical databases
2. Network databases
3. Object-oriented databases
4. Graph databases
5. ER model databases
6. Document databases
7. NoSQL databases
8. Relational databases

1.2.1 Hierarchical Databases

In a hierarchical database management system (hierarchical DBMS) model, data is stored as parent-child relationship nodes. In a hierarchical database, besides actual data, records also include information about their parent/child relationships groups.

In a hierarchical database model, data is organized in a tree-like structure. The data is stored in the form of a collection of fields where each field represents only one value. The records are linked to each other, representing a parent-child relationship. In a hierarchical database model, each child record has only one parent, while a parent can have multiple children.

To retrieve a field's data, we need to traverse through each tree node until that record is found.

The hierarchical database system was developed by IBM in the early 1960s. The hierarchical structure as shown in figure 1.1 is very simple; it is not easy to modify due to the parent-child one-to-many relationship. Hierarchical databases are widely used to build high-performance and availability applications that are usually used in the telecommunications and banking sectors.

The Windows Registry and IBM Information Management System (IMS) are two popular examples of hierarchical databases.

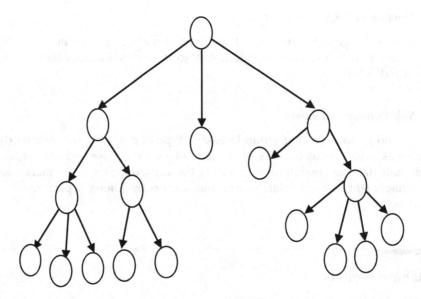

FIGURE 1.1
Hierarchical database.

Advantage

A hierarchical database can be accessed and updated quickly. As shown in the figure above, its model structure is like a tree, and the relationships between records are defined in advance. This feature is a double-edged sword.

Disadvantage

The main disadvantage of this database structure is that each child in the tree can have only one parent. Relationships or linkages between children are not allowed, even if they make sense from a logical point of view. Adding a new field or record requires that the entire database must be redefined.

1.2.2 Network Databases

Network database management systems (network DBMSs) use a network structure to establish relationships between various entities. Network databases are typically used on large digital computers. Network databases are similar to hierarchical databases, but unlike hierarchical databases where one node can have only one parent, a network node can have a relationship with multiple entities. A network database even looks like a cobweb or an interconnected network of records.

In network databases, child nodes are called members and parent nodes are called occupiers. The main difference between each child, or member, is that it can have more than one parent.

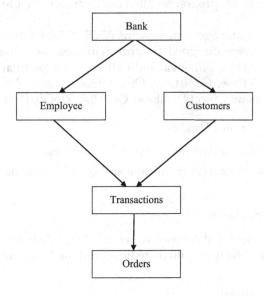

FIGURE 1.2
Network database.

The approval of the network data model as shown in figure 1.2 is very similar to a hierarchical data model. Data in a network database is structured in the form of many-to-many relationships.

This network database structure was invented by Charles Bachman in the late 1960s. Some popular network databases are the Integrated Data Store (IDS), Integrated Database Management System (IDMS), TurboIMAGE, Raima Database Manager, and UNIVAC DMS 1100.

1.2.3 Object-Oriented Model

This model is very similar to the functionality of object-oriented programming. It takes more than the storage of objects in the programming language. Object-oriented model increase the semantics of C++ and Java. It provides full-featured database programming capabilities while containing native language compatibility. It adds the functionalities of the database to object programming languages. Object-oriented model is based on an ana-logical approach to the application and database development into a constant data model and language. It provides benefits, such as the applications require less code, use more natural data modeling, and code bases are much easier to organize. Object developers can write complete database applications with an adequate amount of additional effort.

Object-oriented database derivation is an integral part of object-oriented programming language systems and consistent systems. The main power source for object-oriented data-bases comes from the recurrent treatment of both consistent data, as found in databases, and transient data, as found in executing programs.

Object-oriented databases use small, recyclable entities separated from software called objects. The objects are stored in the object-oriented database.

Each object contains two elements:

1. A piece of data (e.g., sound, video, text, or graphics).
2. Instructions, or software programs called methods, for what to do with the data.

Object-oriented database management systems (OODBMs) were developed in the early 1980s. Some OODBMs were designed to work with object-oriented programming lan-guages such as Ruby, C++, Delphi, Java, and Python. Some popular object-oriented data-bases are TORNADO, VBase, Gemstone, ObjectStore, GBase, Versant Object Database, InterSystems Cache, Versant Object Database, ODABA, ZODB, Poet. JADE, and Informix.

Disadvantages of Object-Oriented Databases

1. Object-oriented databases are more expensive to develop.
2. Most companies are not willing to leave and convert their databases to different forms.

Benefits of Object-Oriented Databases

The benefits of object-oriented databases are enthralling. Their ability to mix and match reusable objects provides the user with incredible multimedia capability.

1.2.4 Graph Databases Model

Graph Databases are one of the NoSQL databases and use a graph structure for processing queries. The data is stored in the form of nodes, edges, and properties between them. In a graph database, a node represents an entity, instance, or an object such as a customer, per-son, or car. Compared to a relational database system, a node is equivalent to a record. An Edge in a graph database shows a relationship that connects nodes. Properties are added to the nodes, which provide additional information for processing a query.

Some popular graph databases are: Neo4j, Azure Cosmos DB, SAP HANA, Sparksee, Oracle Spatial and Graph, OrientDB, ArrangoDB, and MarkLogic. The graph database structure is also supported by some relational database systems, including Oracle and later versions of SQL.

1.2.5 Entity–Relationship Model

An entity–relationship (ER) model is typically implemented as a database model. In a sim-ple relational database system, each row of a table represents one instance of an entity type, and each column in a table represents an attribute type. In a relational database, a relationship is characterized between entities by storing the primary key of one entity as a pointer or "foreign key" in the table of another entity.

The ER model was developed by Peter Chen in 1976.

ER model as shown in figure 1.3 is based on the conviction of real-world entities and relationships among them. The ER model creates entity set, relationship set, general attributes, and constraints formulating the real-world scenarios into the database model.

ER model is best used for conceptual or graphical design of a database.

ER model is based on

- Entities and their *attributes*.
- Relationships among entities.

These concepts are explained below.

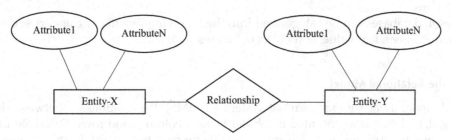

FIGURE 1.3
Entity-relationship diagram.

- Entity: An entity in an ER Model is a real-world entity having various properties known as attributes. Every attribute is defined by its set of values called its domain. For example, in a school database, a student is considered an entity. Here, the student has various attributes like name, age, class, enrolment number, etc.

- Relationship: The logical association between different entities is called a *relationship*. Relationships can be mapped with entities in various ways. Mapping cardinalities declare the number of associations between two entities.

    Mapping cardinalities

  - One-to-one
  - One-to-many
  - Many-to-one
  - Many-to-many

1.2.6 Document Databases Model

Document database (DocumentDB) is also a type of NoSQL database that stores data in the form of documents in the database. Each document represents the data, its relationship with other various data elements, and the attributes of this data. DocumentDB stores data in a key and value form.

DocumentDB has become popular recently due to its NoSQL and document storage properties. NoSQL data storage provides a faster mechanism to store and traverse documents.

Popular NoSQL databases are Cassandra, Hadoop/Hbase, Hypertable, MapR, Cloudera, Hortonworks, Amazon SimpleDB, Apache Flink, IBM Informix, Elastic, MongoDB, and Azure DocumentDB.

1.2.7 NoSQL Databases Model

NoSQL databases do not use SQL as their primary data accessing language. Graph databases, network databases, object databases, and document databases are common types of NoSQL databases.

NoSQL database does not have any predefined schemas, making NoSQL databases a perfect model for rapidly changing development environments.

NoSQL allows developers to make changes in real-timescenarios without affecting applications.

NoSQL databases can be categorized into the following five major categories: column, graph, document, key-value, and object databases.

1.2.8 The Relational Model

In a relational database management system (RDBMS), the relationship between data is relational, and data is represented in tabular form of columns and rows. Each column of a table shows an attribute, and each row in a table represents a record. Each field in a table represents a data record.

Structured Query Language (SQL) is the primary language used to process the query in RDBMS, including inserting, updating, deleting, and searching operations. Relational databases work on each table that has a key field that uniquely indicates each row, which is a primary key. These key fields can be used to connect one primary table to another secondary table.

Relational databases are the most popular and widely used databases of all time. Some popular DDBMS are Oracle, MySQL, SQL Server, SQLite, and IBM DB2.

The relational database has two major advantages:

1. Relational databases can be used with less or nearly no training.
2. Database entries can be modified without modifying the entire body.

The most popular data model in DBMS is the relational model. It is a more scientific model than other database models. This model is based on first-order predicate logic and defines a table as an n-ary relation.

Relational model can be represented as a table with columns and rowsas shown in figure 1.4. Each row is known as a tuple. Each table of the column has a name or attribute.

- **Domain:** It contains a set of atomic values that an attribute can allow.
- **Attribute:** It contains the name of a column of a particular table. Each attribute Ai must have a domain, dom(Ai)
- **Relational instance:** In the relational database system, the relational instance is represented by a finite set of tuples. Relation instances cannot have duplicate tuples.

- **Relational schema:** A relational schema is a structure containing the name of the relation and the name of all columns or attributes.
- **Relational key:** In the relational key, each row has one or more attributes. It can identify the row in the relation uniquely.

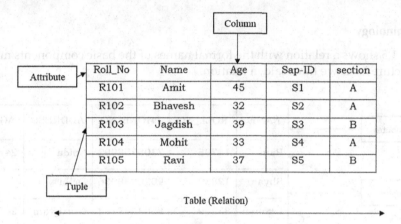

FIGURE 1.4
Relational database example.

The main highlights of this model are

- Data is stored in tables called relations.
- Relations can be easily normalized.
- In normalized relations, values saved are atomic values.
- Each row in a relation contains a unique value.
- Each column in a relation contains values from the same domain.

Properties of Relational Database

In a relational database, we have to follow the properties given below:

a) Name of the relation should be distinct from all other relations.
b) Each relation cell stores exactly one atomic (single) value.
c) Each attribute contains a distinct name.
d) Attribute domain has no significance.
e) Tuple should not have duplicate value.
f) Order of tuples can have a different sequence.

Example: STUDENT Relation

NAME	ROLL_NO	PHONE_NO	ADDRESS	AGE
Ram	14795	7305758992	Noida	24
Shyam	12839	9026288936	Delhi	35
Laxman	33289	8583287182	Gurugram	20
Mahesh	27857	7086819134	Ghaziabad	27
Ganesh	17282	9028 9i3988	Delhi	40

- In the given table, NAME, ROLL_NO, PHONE_NO, ADDRESS, and AGE are the attributes.
- The instance of schema STUDENT has 5 tuples.
- t3 = <Laxman, 33289, 8583287182, Gurugram, 20>

1.2.9 Terminology

The figure 1.5 shows a relation with the formal names of the basic components marked the entire structure is, as we have said, a relation.

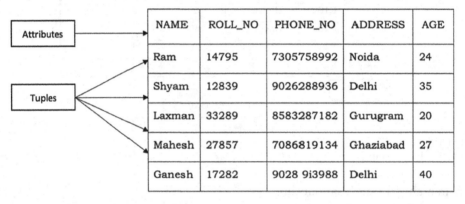

NAME	ROLL_NO	PHONE_NO	ADDRESS	AGE
Ram	14795	7305758992	Noida	24
Shyam	12839	9026288936	Delhi	35
Laxman	33289	8583287182	Gurugram	20
Mahesh	27857	7086819134	Ghaziabad	27
Ganesh	17282	9028 9i3988	Delhi	40

FIGURE 1.5
RDBMS terminology.

Each row of data is a tuple. Actually, each row is an n-tuple, but the "n-" is usually dropped.

Cardinality of a relation: The number of tuples in a relation determines its cardinality. In this case, the relation has a cardinality of 4.

Degree of a relation: Each column in the tuple is called an attribute. The number of attributes in a relation determines its degree. The relation in the figure has a degree of 3.

Domains: A domain definition specifies the kind of data represented by the attribute.

Let's create a table by the student having the following attributes with domains.

Student
```
Rollno varchar(10)
Sapid varchar(10)
Name varchar(10)
City char(10)
Age integer
```

In the above definition, we can see every attribute having a specified domain, like the name having the domain of character only, so it will only accept the character values.

Body of a Relation: The body of the relation includes an unordered set of zero or more tuples. Firstly, the relation is unordered; record numbers do not apply to relations. Secondly, a relation with no tuples still qualifies as a relation. Thirdly, a relation is a set, and the items in a set are uniquely identifiable. Therefore, for a table to qualify as a relation, each record must be uniquely identifiable, and the table should not contain any duplicate records.

Keys of a Relation

It is a set of one or more attributes whose combined values are unique among all occurrences in a given table. A key is the relational means of specifying uniqueness in the table. Some different types of keys are:

Primary key is an attribute or a set of attributes of relation which possess the properties of uniqueness and irreducibility (no subset should be unique). For example, the Supplier number in S table is the primary key, the Part number in P table is the primary key, and the combination of Supplier number and Part number in the SP table is a primary key

Foreign key is the attributes of a table, which points to the primary key of another table. Foreign key permits only those values, which appear in the primary key of the table to which it refers or may be null (unknown value).

Let's take an example where we have two tables account and branch as per the following:

Branch

```
Branchname varchar(20) Primary Key
Branchcity varchar(20)
Code integer
```

Account

```
Accountno varchar(20) Primary Key
Branchname varchar(20)
Balance int
Foreign key(Branchname) references Branch
```

In the above two tables account and branch, we can see that branchname is acting as the primary key in the account table and branchname is acting in the branch table. In the above account table, no records can be added until it's not verified from branch table, so in the account table, branchname acts as foreign key. Account table will act as the child and branch will act as the parent table.

Advantages and Disadvantages of Relational Model

The major advantages of the relational model are:

Structural independence: In relational model, creating any changes in the database structure does not affect the data access. Structural independence can be achieved when it is possible to change the database structure without affecting the DBMS's capability to access data. So, the relational database model has structural independence as a major advantage.

Conceptual simplicity: We have seen that both the hierarchical and the network database models were very simple conceptually. But the relational database model is even simpler at the conceptual level compared to these models. In the relational model, the designers can concentrate on the logical view of the database as the model frees the designer from the physical data storage details.

Design, implementation, maintenance, and usage ease: The relational database model achieves both data independence and structure independence, as a result, making the database design, administration, maintenance, and usage much easier than the other models.

Ad hoc query capability: The main reason for the immense popularity of the relational database model is the presence of very powerful, flexible, and easy-to-use query capability. The query language of the relational database models, structured query language or SQL, helps in making ad hoc queries a reality. SQL is a fourth-generation language. It allows the user to specify what must be done without specifying how it should be performed. So, the users can specify what information they want and leave details of how to get the information to the database.

Disadvantages of Relational Model

The relational model's disadvantages are very less compared to the advantages, and their capabilities far outweigh the cons. Also, the drawbacks of the relational database systems could be avoided if proper corrective and avoidance measures are adopted. The main reason for these drawbacks is not because of the shortcomings in the database model but the way it is being implemented.

Some of the disadvantages are:

Hardware overheads: Relational database system hides the implementation processes, complexities, and the physical data storage details of the database from the users. To make things easier for the users, the relational database systems need more powerful hardware computers and data storage devices to run smoothly. But, as the processing power of servers is increasing at a rapid rate, so the need for more processing power is no longer a very huge issue.

Ease of design can lead to bad design: The relational database is an easy design model and easy to use. The users don't need to know the complex details of physical data storage. They need not know how the data is actually stored in a database. As a result, this ease of design and use can lead to the development and implementation of very poorly designed database management model. Since the database is efficient, these design inefficiencies will not come to light when there is only a small amount of data. If the database grows, these poorly designed databases will slow down the system and result in performance reduction and data corruption.

'Information island' phenomenon: As discussed earlier, relational database systems are easier to implement and use. This will create a situation where too many people or departments try to create their databases and applications.

These information islands will prevent the information integration required for the smooth and efficient functioning of a company. These individual databases will also develop problems like data inconsistency, duplication, redundancy and many more issues.

But as we have discussed, these issues are minor compared to the advantages, and all these issues could be avoided if the organization has a properly designed database and good avoidance database standards.

1.3 Database Languages

Database languages are used to perform a variety of complex tasks that help a DBMS function correctly. These tasks can be query processing operations such as read, update, insert, search, or delete the data stored in the database. Different types of database languages and the various operations that these languages can perform on the data are:

Types of Database Languages

The data languages are categorized into four different types based on the various operations performed by the language. These include:

1.3.1 Data Definition Language (DDL)

Data Definition Language (DDL) is a set of special commands that allows us to define and modify the structure and schema of the database. These commands can be used to create, delete, and modify the database structures such as tables, schema, indexes, etc. DDL commands can alter the structure of the whole database, and every change implemented by a DDL command is auto-committed (the change that is permanently saved in the database); these commands are normally not used by an end user or someone who is accessing the database via an application.

The most common DDL commands are

- Create – Use to create a relation/table.
- Alter – Used to modify the structure of a relation.
- Drop – Used to delete a relation with its structure
- Rename – Used to rename of relation.

Note: DDL commands are auto-committed, so we need not commit separately.

1.3.2 Data Manipulation Language (DML)

Data manipulation language (DML) is a set of special commands that allows us to access and manipulate data already stored in an existing relation/table. These commands are used to perform certain operations, such as insertion, updation, deletion, and retrieval of the data from the database. These commands work based on user requests as they are responsible for all types of data modification. The Data manipulation language commands that deal with retrieving the data are known as Data Query Language.

NOTE: The DML commands are not auto-committed, i.e., the changes and modifications done via these commands can be rolled back.

DML commands are:

- Insert Into – Used to insert a or multiple records in a relation.
- Delete – Delete a or multiple records that satisfy a given condition.
- Update – Update the values of a records already in a relation.

1.3.3 Data Control Language (DCL)

Data Control Language (DCL) is a set of special commands used to control the user authorities and privileges in the database system. The user privileges include ALL, CREATE, SELECT, INSERT, UPDATE, DELETE, EXECUTE, etc.

A user requires data access permissions to process any command or query in the database system. This user access is controlled using the DCL commands. These statements are used to grant and revoke the authority of the user to access the data or the database.

DCL commands are transactional, i.e., these commands include rollback parameters.

Transaction Control Language (TCL) is a set of special commands that deal with all the transactions within the database. A transaction is a collection of sequential tasks treated as a single execution unit by the DBMS software. Hence, transactions are responsible for executing different tasks simultaneously within a database.

The modifications performed using the DML commands can be executed or rollbacked with the help of TCL commands. These commands are used to check on other commands and their consequences on the database.

1.3.4 Data Retrieval Language (DRL)

Data Retrieval Language will be used to retrieve the records already stored in a database.

SELECT FROM: Show you how to use a simple SELECT FROM statement to query the data from a single table.

The SELECT statement allows you to select data from one or more tables. To write a SELECT statement in MySQL, you use this syntax:

```
Select name from student;
```

SELECT: Learn how to use the SELECT statement without referencing a table.

MySQL doesn't require the FROM clause. It means that you can have a SELECT statement without the FROM clause as below:

> Query: Select 1+1;
>
> Output: 2

> Query: select datetime;
>
> Output: display the current date and time

> Query: Select concat 'Jag' +'dish';
>
> Output: Join the string and show the result Jagdish

Sometimes, we use the FROM clause but do not reference any actual table. In this case, we can use the dual table in the FROM clause:

> Query: Select 1+1 from dual;
>
> Output: 2

The dual table is a shadow/dummy table, not an actual table.

1.4 SQL: A Nonprocedural Language

SQL is a database access language that is both simple and powerful. SQL is a nonprocedural language. The users who use it to explain what they want to be done in SQL, and the SQL language compiler constructs a procedure automatically to browse the database and complete the operation.

SQL *statements* are used to perform all operations on information stored in an Oracle Database. A valid SQL *command* is represented by a SQL *statement*. A statement is made up in part of SQL *reserved words*, which will have a specific meaning in SQL and can't be used for anything else. SELECT and UPDATE, for example, are reserved words that cannot be used as table names.

A SQL statement is indeed a relatively simple but extremely powerful computer software program or instruction. The statement must be the same as a SQL "sentence," for example, SELECT name, city FROM student;

1.4.1 MySQL

MySQL is a relational database management system based on the Structured Query Language (SQL), the most often used language for accessing and managing database records. Under the GNU licensing, MySQL is open source and free software backed up by Oracle Company.

MySQL is the most widely used DBMS software for managing relational databases today. Oracle Corporation supports this open source database software. Compared to Microsoft SQL Server and Oracle Database, it is a quick, scalable, and user-friendly DBMS. It's frequently combined with PHP scripts to build powerful and dynamic server-side or web-based enterprise applications.

MySQL is a RDBMS that can perform the following tasks:

- It allows us to perform database operations on tables, rows, columns, and indexes.
- It defines database relationships as tables (collection of rows and columns), also referred to as relations.
- It ensures that rows or columns in different tables have the same referential integrity.
- It allows us to update the table indexes automatically.
- It extensively uses SQL queries and integrates important data from several columns for end-users.

How MySQL Works?

MySQL is based on the working of client-server architecture. This model is designed for the end users known as clients to access the resources from a central computer known as a server using network services. Here, the clients send requests through a graphical user interface (GUI), and the server will give the desired output as soon as the instructions are processed. The procedure of the MySQL environment is the same as the client-server model.

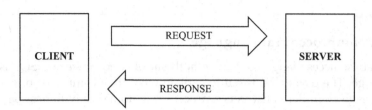

FIGURE 1.6
MySQL structure.

The core of the MySQL database is the MySQL Server. This server is available as a separate program and is responsible for handling all the database statements, instructions, or commands. The working of MySQL database with MySQL server is as follows:

1. MySQL creates a database that allows the users to build various tables to store and manipulate data and define the relationship between each table.
2. Clients make requests through the GUI screen or command prompt using specific SQL queries on the MySQL server.
3. Finally, the server application will process the query, respond with the requested expressions and display the desired result on the client-side.

A client can use any MySQL interface as depicted in figure 1.6. It is responsible for ensuring that the GUI should be lighter and user-friendly to make your data management activities faster and smoother. Some of the most widely used MySQL GUIs are MySQL Workbench, and Sequel Pro, etc.

Reasons for Popularity

Main reasons that MySQL is so popular these days are:

- MySQL is an open source database; as a result, we don't have to pay a single penny to use it.
- MySQL is a very powerful program and can handle a large set of complex functionality of the most expensive and powerful database packages.
- MySQL is easily customizable because it is an open source database open for all, and the open source GPL license facilitates programmers to modify the SQL software according to their specific requirements.
- MySQL is faster than other databases, so it can work well even with large data sets.
- MySQL can support many operating systems with many languages like PHP, PERL, C, C++, JAVA, etc.
- MySQL uses a standard format of the well-known SQL data language.
- MySQL is very much friendly with PHP language, the most popular language for web development.
- MySQL can support large databases, even up to 50 million rows or more in a table. The default file size limit for a table is 4 GB, but you can increase this to a theoretical limit of 8 million terabytes (TB).

1.4.2 SQL Examples

Question: Create an employee database with the basic details for an employee

```
Create table employee
(
Empid varchar(10),
Empname varchar(10),
Dept varchar(10),
Deptid integer,
City char(10),
DOJ Date,
DOB Date
)
```

Output:

Table Created

- SELECT FROM: Show you how to use a simple SELECT FROM statement to query the data from a single table.

  The SELECT statement allows you to select data from one or more tables. To write a SELECT statement in MySQL, you use this syntax:

```
Select name from student;
```

- SELECT: Learn how to use the SELECT statement without referencing a table.

  MySQL doesn't require the FROM clause. It means that you can have a SELECT statement without the FROM clause as below:

  Query: Select 1+1;
  Output: 2

  Query: select datetime;
  Output: display the current date and time

  Query: Select concat 'Jag' +'dish';
  Output: Join the string and show the result Jagdish

  Sometimes, we use the FROM clause but do not reference any actual table. In this case, we can use the dual table in the FROM clause:

  Query: Select 1+1 from dual;
  Output: 2

The dual table is a shadow/dummy table, not an actual table.

1.5 Data Types in SQL

A database table contains multiple columns with particular data types. MySQL provides many data types other than just numeric and string. Every data type in MySQL can be set on by the following characteristics:

- The type of values it represents.
- The amount of space that takes up and whether the values are a constant length or variable length.
- The values of the data type can be indexed or non-indexed.
- How MySQL differentiates between the values of a specific data types shown in Table 1.1.

TABLE 1.1

SQL Data Types

Data Type	Spec.
Char	String (0–255)
Varchar	String (0–255)
Tinytext	String (0–255)
Text	String (0–65535)
MediumText	String (0–16777215)
LongText	String (0–4294967295)
TinyInt	Integer (−128 to 127)
SmallInt	Integer (−32768 to 32767)
MediumInt	Integer (−8388608 to 8388607)
Int	Integer (−2147483648 to 2147483647)
BigInt	Integer (−9223372036854775808 to 9223372036854775807)
Float	Decimal (precise to 23 digits)
Double	Decimal (24 to 53 digits)
Decimal	Double stored as string
Date	YYYY-MM-DD
dateTime	YYYYMMDDHHMMSS
Time	HH:MM:SS

SQL Numeric Data Types

SQL standard numeric types, including exact number data types and approximate numeric data types, including integer, fixed-point, and floating-point. In addition, numeric types can be signed or unsigned except for the BIT type.

The following Table 1.2 shows the summary of numeric types in MySQL:

TABLE 1.2

Numeric Data Types

Numeric Types	Description
TINYINT	A very small integer
SMALLINT	A small integer
MEDIUMINT	A medium-sized integer
INT	A standard integer
BIGINT	A large integer
DECIMAL	A fixed-point number
FLOAT	A single-precision floating point number
DOUBLE	A double-precision floating point number
BIT	A bit field

SQL String Data Types

In MySQL, a string can hold anything from plain text to binary data. Strings can be differentiated and searched based on pattern matching using the LIKE operator and full-text search.

The following Table 1.3 shows the string data types:

TABLE 1.3

String Data Types

String Types	Descriptions
CHAR	A fixed-length nonbinary (character) string
VARCHAR	A variable-length nonbinary string
BINARY	A fixed-length binary string
TINYTEXT	A very small nonbinary string
TEXT	A small nonbinary string
MEDIUMTEXT	A medium-sized nonbinary string
LONGTEXT	A large nonbinary string

SQL Date and Time Data Types

MySQL provides types for date and time. In addition, MySQL supports the timestamp data type for tracking the changes in a row of a table. If you just want to store years without dates and months, you can use the YEAR data type.

The following Table 1.4 illustrates the MySQL date and time data types:

TABLE 1.4

Date Time Data Types

Date and Time Types	Description
DATE	A date value in CCYY-MM-DD format
TIME	A time value in HH:MM:SS format
DATETIME	A date and time value in CCYY-MM-DD HH:MM:SS format
TIMESTAMP	A time stamp value in CCYY-MM-DD HH:MM:SS format
YEAR	A year value in CCYY or YY format

JSON Data Type

MySQL has supported a native JSON data type since version 5.7.8, allowing us to store and manage JSON documents more effectively. The native JSON data type provides automatic validation of JSON documents and optimal storage format.

1.6 Creating Database

The CREATE DATABASE statement creates a new database. The following is an example of the CREATE DATABASE statement:

```
Create database database_Name;
```

> Example: Create database University;
> Output: Database created

Within an instance of SQL Server the name of the database should be unique. It must also comply with the SQL Server identifier's rules. Usually, the database name has a limit of 128 characters.

```
Use database database_name;
```

> Example: Use University;

Once the statement executes successfully, you can view the newly created database.

1.7 Use of MySQL

MySQL is a RDBMS that works on SQL queries. SQL is one of the most popular languages for accessing and managing the records in the table. MySQL is under the GNU licensee's. It is open source and free-to-use software. Oracle Company supports it.

Benefits of MySQL

The benefits are enlisted below:

1. **Easy to use:** As it supports SQL language, user doesn't need any technical expertise to access the database. Users with basic SQL knowledge can easily access database with experience with other relational databases.

2. **Cost free:** Being free of cost users don't have to spend any money for the license.

3. **Customizable code:** Being an open source tool, its source code is freely available to web users. Software developers have an option to customize the source code as per their own applications and use it. The do's and don'ts of the software are defined in **GPL**, i.e., GNU General Public License.

4. **Secured:** It is used by many well-known applications like Facebook, Twitter, etc., as it is one of the most secured databases in the world. Its various security features like **Firewall, Encryption**, and **User Authentication** help protect sensitive user information from intruders.

5. **Better performance:** It supports the multi-engine storage feature, which facilitates database administrators to configure the database to balance the workload. Hence, it makes the database flawless in terms of performance.

6. **High Availability:** It offers 24*7 hours availability and solutions like **Master/Slave Replication** and specialized **Cluster Servers**.

7. **Scalability:** It offers very good scalability to web applications through **MySQL Thread Pool** provided by MySQL Enterprise Edition. Thread pool uses a model that is similar to the multi-user connections overhead for managing threads (processes) in a hassle-free way.

8. **Platform-Friendly:** It is a platform-friendly database supporting several platforms like Microsoft Windows, Oracle Solaris, AIX, Symbian, Linux, MAC OS, etc.

9. **Friendly Interface:** It has a user-friendly interface with many self-management features and different automated processes like configuration and administration-related tasks.

MySQL Uses

Let's have a look at highlighted features of this database like **data security, high availability, and cloud service** in detail to understand why it is a preferred database?

Security

The very next step after the creation of a database is to identify the threats to the security of the database and formulate a security policy before giving access to the database users. Data security is considered to be a necessary feature to look upon. That's why it is being trusted by the world's most popular and huge web applications like Facebook, Twitter, Instagram, Joomla, etc. It offers various safeguard features that stand by the database and prevent breaching.

Security Features of MySQL

- **MySQL Enterprise Firewall**
  Enterprise Firewall protects databases against security threats, such as SQL Injection, Sniffing Attack, or Trojan horse. It monitors the database constantly, sends alerts if an attack is observed, and even blocks any suspicious or unauthorized activity. It prepares a white list of approved SQL statements according to which it measures the authenticity of user activity on the database.

- **MySQL Enterprise Encryption**
  Encryption is a data securing process through which confidential and sensitive data can be encoded, and only authorized users can decode the same. It offers the provision of encrypting data through the Public Key Cryptography feature. **MySQL Enterprise Encryption facilitates:**

  - Data encryption using RSA, DSA, or DH algorithms.

  - Key generation to perform data encryption and decryption.

  - Digital signature to authenticate senders.

  - Avoids data exposure by authorizing DBAs to manage encrypted information.

- **MySQL Transparent Data Encryption (TDE)**
  MySQL TDE provides better security features by encrypting critical information at the physical data files level. Physical files of the database get encrypted even before data gets written to physical storage devices, and they only get decrypted during the reading process. This prevents hackers or malicious users from accessing sensitive data without actual access.

- **User Authentication**
  Different user authentication modules, like Windows Active Directory or Linux Pluggable Authentication Modules (PAM), have been offered by the Enterprise Edition that can be easily plugged in with the existing applications to improve their security by maintaining a centralized directory. This feature eliminates the need to maintain the user's details within individual systems.

- **MySQL Enterprise Audit**
  This is an Enterprise solution that performs auditing based on predefined policies. The audit is being performed to track user activity in order to keep a check on control security and prevent misuse of information. **This solution allows administrators to**

  - Enable or disable the audit stream.

  - Customize policies to perform logging for all or selected user activities.

  - Perform integration of XML-based audit log file with MySQL, Oracle, or other solutions.

- **InnoDB Transactional Support**
  MySQL storage engine InnoDB supports ACID-compliant transactions within the database to ensure its security. Features like multiversion concurrency control (MVCC), maintaining database snapshots at different points of time, and implementing foreign keys help in maintaining database integrity.

- **MySQL online backup**
  Using **online backup**, database backups can be taken while the database is an inactive state. Along with "hot" or "online" backup, it allows full, partial, incremental, or selective backups. It also allows database recovery using the "point-in-time recovery" (PITR) method.

1.8 Summary

A database is a tool for collecting, storing, manipulating, and organizing information. Databases can store information about students, employees, people, products, orders, or critical data. Many databases start as a list in a word-processing program or spreadsheet. As the list grows, redundancies and inconsistencies begin to increase in the data. The data becomes hard to understand in a list format, and there are limited ways of searching or pulling subsets of data out for review. Once these problems start to appear, the best way to avoid such problems is to transfer the data to a database created by a DBMS. RDBMS is the most widely used database where data is represented in the form of rows and columns. For managing the RDBMS, we are using database languages, and several types of data types are used in the processing of the database. To get the maximum efficiency out of a database, the data needs to be organized into tables to avoid redundancies. For example, if you're storing information about employees, details of each employee should only need to be entered once in a table set up just to hold employee data. Data about products will be stored in its own table, and data about branch and offices will be stored in another individual table.

Each row in a table is referred to as a record. Records are where the individual section of information is stored. Each record consists of one or more fields. Fields correspond to the columns in the table. For example, you might have a table named "employees" where each record (row) contains information about a different employee, and each field (column) contains a different type of information, such as first name, last name, address, and so on. Fields must be designated as a certain data type, whether it's text, date or time, number, or some other type.

References

1. Patni, J.C., Sharma, H.K., Tomar, R., & Katal, A. (2022). *Database Management System: An Evolutionary Approach* (1st ed.). Chapman and Hall/CRC. https://doi.org/10.1201/9780429 282843
2. 'What Is a Database', [online]. Available: https://www.oracle.com/in/database/what-is-database/#:~:text=A%20database%20is%20an%20organized,database%20management%20system%20(DBMS), [Accessed: 25 April 2022].
3. 'Differece between Database and Spreadsheet', [online]. Available: https://www.hivewire.co/blog-post/database-vs-spreadsheet, [Accessed: 25 April 2022].
4. 'Benefits of Databases', [online]. Available: https://www.nibusinessinfo.co.uk/content/types-database-system, [Accessed: 20 April 2022].
5. 'SQL Data Types', [online]. Available: https://www.journaldev.com/16774/sql-data-types, [Accessed: 04 April 2022].
6. 'Data Models', [online]. Available: https://www.tutorialspoint.com/dbms/dbms_data_models.htm, [Accessed: 01 April 2022].
7. 'Relational Database', [online]. Available: https://www.techtarget.com/searchdatamanagement/definition/relational-database, [Accessed: 20 April 2022].
8. 'Database Languages', [online]. Available: https://www.scaler.com/topics/databse-languages-in-dbms/, [Accessed: 20 January 2022].

9. 'DDL & DML', [online]. Available: https://web.csulb.edu/colleges/coe/cecs/dbdesign/dbdesign.php?page=sql/ddldml.php, [Accessed: 07 April 2022].
10. 'SQL Data Types', [online]. Available: http://www-db.deis.unibo.it/courses/TW/DOCS/w3schools/sql/sql_datatypes_general.asp.html, [Accessed: 17 April 2022].
11. 'SQL Data Types', [online]. Available: https://www.vertica.com/docs/9.2.x/HTML/Content/Authoring/SQLReferenceManual/DataTypes/SQLDataTypes.htm, [Accessed: 17 May 2022].

2

Creating and Manipulating Database

Creating and manipulating the database will be discussed in the following topics:

1. Data Definition Languages
2. Data Manipulation Language

2.1 Data Definition Language (DDL)

Data definition language (DDL) is a set of special commands that allows us to define and modify the structure and metadata of the database. These commands can be used to create, modify, and delete the database structures such as schema, tables, indexes, etc. DDL commands can alter the structure of the whole database, and every change implemented by a DDL command is auto-committed (the change is saved permanently in the database); these commands are normally not used by an end user (someone who is accessing the database via an application).

The most common DDL commands are:

- Create
- Alter
- Drop
- Truncate
- Rename

2.1.1 Create Command

This command is used to create the relation/table as per the specifications and constraints. Before creating relation, we can alternatively create and use the database.

Syntax

Create database database_name (is used to create a new database)

Use Database_name(is used to use the created database)

Create table Syntax

```
Create table table_name
(
Attribute1 datatype size,
Attribute2 datatype size,
.

.

.

AttributeN datatype size
);
Example create table
Create table student
(
Rollno varchar(10),
Sapid varchar(10),
Name char(20),
City char(20)
);
```

Output

```
Table created.
```

The above will create a student table having the attributes rollno, sapid, name, and city. After creating the table, we can see the structure of the table by the following command

```
Desc student;
```

This will show the following result in Table 2.1.

TABLE 2.1

Student

Column	Null?	Type
ROLLNO	—	VARCHAR2(10)
SAPID	—	VARCHAR2(10)
NAME	—	CHAR(20)
CITY	—	CHAR(10)

2.1.2 ALTER Command

This command is used to modify the structure of the relation by adding a new column, dropping an existing column, modifying the size of the column, and changing the name of the column.

Add Column Syntax: It is used to add a new column I the exiting table.

```
Alter table table_name
Add column_name datatype size;
```

Example

```
Alter table student
Add fname char(10);
```

Output

```
Table altered.
```

drop Column Syntax: It is used to drop a column from an existing table.

```
Alter table table_name
drop column column_name;
```

Example

```
Alter table student
Drop column city;
```

Output

```
Table altered.
```

Modify Column: This is used to change the data type and size of the data type.

```
Alter table table_name
Modify column_name datatype size;
```

Example

```
Alter table student
Modify fname varchar(20);
```

Output

```
Table altered.
```

2.1.3 DROP Command

It is used to delete the complete relation with its structure.

DROP Syntax

```
Drop table table_name;
```

Example

```
Drop table student;
```

Output

```
Table dropped.
```

2.1.4 TRUNCATE Command

It is used to remove the whole content of the table along with the deallocation of the space occupied by the data without affecting the table's structure.

Syntax

```
Truncate table table_name;
```

Example

```
Truncate table student;
```

Output

```
Table truncated.
```

Note: We can also use the DROP command to delete the complete table, but the DROP command will remove the structure along with the contents of the table. Hence, if we want to remove the data present inside a table, not the table itself, we can use TRUNCATE instead of DROP.

2.1.5 Rename Command

It is used to change the name of an existing table or a database object.

Syntax

```
Rename old_table_name to new_table_name;
```

Example

```
Rename student to student2022;
```

Output

```
Statement processed.
```

To rename a column of a table:

```
Alter table table_name
Rename column old_Column_name to new_Column_name;
```

Example

```
Alter table student
Rename column name to stuname;
```

Output

```
Table altered.
```

2.2 Data Manipulation Language (DML)

Data manipulation language (DML) is a set of special commands that allows us to access and manipulate data stored in existing relation/table. These commands are used to perform certain operations, such as insertion, deletion, updation, and retrieval of the data from the database. These commands deal with the user requests as they are responsible for all types of data modification. The DML commands that deal with retrieving the data are known as Data Query language.

Note: The DML commands are not auto-committed, i.e., the changes and modifications done via these commands can be rolled back.

DML commands are:

- Insert Into
- Delete
- Update
- Select

2.2.1 INSERT INTO Command

This command is used to insert the records in a relation.

Syntax

```
Insert into table_name values (attribute1 value, attribute2 value,..........
attributeN value)
                              Or
Insert into table_name (attribute1, attribute2,..........attributeN)
Values(value1, value2,..............valueN);
```

Example

```
Insert into student values ('A11012', 'S23467','Rakesh','Haldwani');
                              Or
Insert into student (Rollno,sapid,name,city)
Values('A11012', 'S23467','Rakesh','Haldwani')
```

Output

```
1 row(s) inserted.
```

Note: While using the INSERT INTO command, ensure that the data types of each column match the inserted value, as this may lead to unexpected scenarios and errors in the database.

2.2.2 DELETE Command

This command is used to delete the one or multiple records that are satisfying the given predicate.

Syntax

```
Delete from table_name where (condition)
```

Example

```
Delete from student where rollno='1';
```

Output

```
1 row(s) deleted.
```

While deleting records from a table, we have to ensure that the proper condition is applied or not; otherwise; we can lose the records.

For example, we have to delete a record of a student whose name is Amit and rollno is 1; in such cases, we have to use rollno attribute in condition as it is unique due to the primary key. If we use the name attribute in the condition, all the records will be deleted whose name is Amit.

Note: The DELETE statement only removes the data from the table, whereas the TRUNCATE statement also frees the memory along with data removal. Hence, TRUNCATE is more efficient in removing all the data from a table.

2.2.3 Update Command

This command is used to modify the existing records by updating the values of their attributes.

Syntax

```
Update table_name
Set columnname=new value where (condition)
```

Example

```
Update student
Set name='Rakesh Kumar' where rollno=1;
```

Output

```
1 row(s) updated.
```

Multiple records will be updated if we are not applying any condition.

```
Update student
Set name='Rakesh Kumar';
```

```
5 row(s) updated.
```

Note: Here, the SET statement is used to set new values to the particular column and WHERE clause is used to select rows for which the columns are updated for the given table.

2.2.4 SELECT Command

SELECT command is used to retrieve one or many records per the given condition.

Syntax

```
Select * from table_name
```

Will display all the records from the table with the above select query.

Example

```
Select * from student;
```

Output Shown in the table 2.2

TABLE 2.2

Student Table after DML Operations

ROLLNO	SAPID	NAME	CITY
1	S01	Ajay Kumar Sharma	Ghaziabad
2	S02	Chetan	Delhi
3	S03	Rakesh	Haldwani
4	S04	Jagdish	Dehradun
5	S05	Archana	Sitapur

```
Select name, sapid from student;
```

This query will select the values of name and sapid from the student table.

Output Shown in the table 2.3

TABLE 2.3

Select Operation on Student Table

NAME	SAPID
Ajay Kumar Sharma	S01
Chetan	S02
Rakesh	S03
Jagdish	S04
Archana	S05

```
Select name from student where Rollno>='3';
```

This will display the name values of all those records whose rollno value is greater than or equal to 3.

Output Shown in the table 2.4

TABLE 2.4

Select Operation with Where Clause on Student Table

NAME
Chetan
Jagdish
Archana

Highlights

1. Set of commands is used to access and manipulate data stored in existing schema objects.

2. All changes done by DML commands can be rolled back.

3. DML statements deal with the user requests.

4. Examples – SELECT, INSERT, UPDATE, DELETE

2.3 Data Control Language (DCL)

Data control language (DCL) is a set of special commands used to control the user privileges in the database system. The user privileges include ALL, CREATE, SELECT, INSERT, UPDATE, DELETE, EXECUTE, etc.

We require data access permissions to execute any command or query in the database system. This user access is controlled using the DCL statements. These statements grant and revoke user access to data or the database.

DCL commands are transactional, i.e., these commands include rollback parameters. These commands include:

Grant:

It is used to provide user access to the database or its objects.

Syntax

To grant user privilege to specified users on a database object:

```
GRANT <privilege>ON <table_name> TO user1, user2;
```

Revoke:

It is used to revoke user access to the database system.

Syntax

To revoke user privilege to specified users on a database object:

```
REVOKE <privilege>ON <table_name>FROM user1, user2;
```

Note: In practical usage, instead of having a separate language for every operation, a combination of DDL, DML, and DCL is used as part of a single database language such as SQL.

Highlights

1. Set of commands is used to control the user privileges in the database system.
2. The user privileges include ALL, CREATE, SELECT, INSERT, UPDATE, DELETE, EXECUTE, etc.
3. DCL commands are transactional.
4. Examples—GRANT, REVOKE
5. In practice, a combination of DDL, DML, and DCL is used as a single database language.

2.4 Transaction Control Language (TCL)

Transaction control language (TCL) is a set of special commands, dealing with the transactions within the database. A transaction is a collection of related tasks treated as a single execution unit by the DBMS software. Hence, transactions are responsible for executing different tasks within a database.

The modifications performed using the DML commands are executed or roll backed with the help of TCL commands. These commands are used to keep a check on other commands and their effects on the database. These include:

COMMIT

It saves all the modifications permanently done (all the transactions) by the DML commands in the database. Once issued, it cannot be undone.

DBMS software implicitly uses the COMMIT command before and after every DDL command to save the change permanently in the database.

Syntax

```
COMMIT;
```

ROLLBACK

It is used to undo the transactions that have not already been permanently saved (or committed) to the database.

It restores the previously stored value, i.e., the data present before the execution of the transactions.

Syntax   To undo a group of transactions since last COMMIT or SAVEPOINT:

```
ROLLBACK;
```

To undo a group of transactions to a certain point:

```
ROLLBACK TO savepoint_name;
```

SAVEPOINT

It is used to create a point within the groups of transactions to save or roll back later.

It is used to roll the transactions back to a certain point without the need to roll back the whole group of transactions.

Syntax   To create a SAVEPOINT:

```
SAVEPOINT savepoint_name;
```

To release a SAVEPOINT:

```
RELEASE SAVEPOINT savepoint_name;
```

AUTOCOMMIT

It is used to enable/disable the auto-commit process that commits each transaction after its execution.

Syntax   To enable the AUTOCOMMIT process:

```
SET AUTOCOMMIT = 1 ;
```

To disable the AUTOCOMMIT process:

```
SET AUTOCOMMIT = 0;
```

Highlights

1. Set of commands that deal with the transactions within the database.
2. Used to keep a check on other commands and their effects on the database.
3. A transaction is a group of related tasks, treated as a single execution unit.
4. Examples—COMMIT, ROLLBACK, SAVEPOINT, AUTOCOMMIT.

2.5 Database Structure

Database management system (DBMS) acts as an interface between the user and the database. The user requests the DBMS to perform various operations (insert, delete, update, and retrieval) on the database. The components of DBMS perform these requested operations on the database and provide necessary data to the users. The various components of DBMS are shown below in Figure 2.1:

1. DDL Compiler: Data description language compiler processes schema definitions specified in the DDL. It includes metadata information, such as the name of the files, data items, storage details of each file, mapping information and constraints, etc.

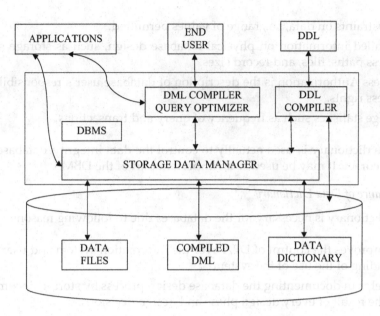

FIGURE 2.1
Structure of DBMS.

2. DML Compiler and Query optimizer: The DML commands such as insert, update, delete, and retrieve from the application program are sent to the DML compiler for compilation into object code for database access. The object code is then optimized in the best way to execute a query by the query optimizer and then sent to the data manager.

3. Data Manager: The data manager is the central software component of the DBMS, also known as database control system.

    The main functions of data manager are:

    • Convert operations in user's queries coming from the application programs or combination of DML compiler and query optimizer, which is known as query processor from user's logical view to the physical file system.

    • Controls DBMS information access that is stored on disk.

    • It also controls handling buffers in the main memory.

    • It also enforces constraints to maintain the consistency and integrity of the data.

    • It also synchronizes the simultaneous operations performed by the concurrent users.

    • It also controls the backup and recovery operations.

4. Data Dictionary: Data dictionary is a repository of description of data in the database. It contains information about

    • Data: names of the tables, names of attributes of each table, length of attributes, and number of rows in each table.

    • Relationships between database transactions and data items referenced are useful in determining which transactions are affected when certain data definitions are changed.

- Constraints on data, i.e., range of values permitted.
- Detailed information on physical database design, such as storage structure, access paths, files, and record sizes.
- Access Authorization is the description of database user's responsibilities and access rights.
- Usage statistics such as frequency of query and transactions.

Data dictionary is used actually to control the data integrity, database operation, and accuracy. It may be used as an important part of the DBMS.

Importance of Data Dictionary

Data dictionary is necessary for the databases due to following reasons:

- It improves the control of DBA over the information system and user's understanding of the use of the system.
- It helps in documenting the database design process by storing documentation of the result of every design phase and design decisions.
- It helps in searching the views on the database definitions of those views.
- It provides great assistance in producing a report on which data elements (i.e., data values) are used in all the programs.
- It promotes data independence, i.e., by adding or modifying structures in the database application program that are not affected.
5. Data Files: It contains the data portion of the database.
6. Compiled DML: The DML complier converts the high-level queries into low-level file access commands known as compiled DML.
7. End Users: They are already discussed in the previous section.

2.6 Examples

Question: Create an employee table with the relevant set of the attribute.

```
Create table employee
(
Empid varchar(10),
Empname varchar(10),
Dept varchar(10),
Deptid integer,
City char(10),
DOJ Date,
DOB Date
);
```

Output:

Table Created

Question: Show the structure of the above-created table.

```
Desc employee;
```

Output Shown in the table 2.5

TABLE 2.5

Employee

Column	Null?	Type
EMPID	–	VARCHAR2(10)
EMPNAME	–	VARCHAR2(10)
DEPT	–	VARCHAR2(10)
DEPTID	–	NUMBER
CITY	–	CHAR(10)
DOJ	–	DATE
DOB	–	DATE

Question: Add a new attribute deptno to the employee table.
Answer: For adding a new attribute, we will use the alter command as below;

```
Alter table employee
Add deptno Integer;
```

Output Shown in the table 2.6

Table altered

If we want to see either the attribute added or not, we have to check again the desc command that will show the complete structure of the table.

TABLE 2.6

Employee after Adding a Column

Column	Null?	Type
EMPID	—	VARCHAR2(10)
EMPNAME	—	VARCHAR2(10)
DEPT	—	VARCHAR2(10)
DEPTID	—	NUMBER
CITY	—	CHAR(10)
DOJ	—	DATE
DOB	—	DATE
DEPTNO	—	NUMBER

Question: Remove the attribute city from the employee table.
Answer: We will use the alter command to delete the attribute as below

```
Alter table employee
Drop column city;
```

Output Shown in the table 2.7

Table altered

TABLE 2.7

Employee after Dropping a Column

Column	Null?	Type
EMPID	—	VARCHAR2(10)
EMPNAME	—	VARCHAR2(10)
DEPT	—	VARCHAR2(10)
DEPTID	—	NUMBER
DOJ	—	DATE
DOB	—	DATE
DEPTNO	—	NUMBER

Question: Change the type and size of the empid in the employee table.

Answer: Here, we will use the modify command with alter command as below.

```
Alter table employee
Modify empid number;
```

Output Shown in the table 2.8

Table altered

TABLE 2.8

Employee after Modify a Column

Column	Null?	Type
EMPID	—	NUMBER
EMPNAME	—	VARCHAR2(10)
DEPT	—	VARCHAR2(10)
DEPTID	—	NUMBER
DOJ	—	DATE
DOB	—	DATE
DEPTNO	—	NUMBER

Question: Erase the complete data from the employee table.

Answer: To erase the complete data from the table, we will use the truncate command that will erase all the data from the table, but the structure will remain in the database.

```
Truncate table employee;
```

Output:

Table truncated

Question: Erase the complete data with its structure of employee data.

Answer: We will use the drop command that will delete the complete table with its structure.

```
Drop table employee;
```

Output:

Table dropped

Question: Insert the eight records in the employee table.
Answer: We will use the Insert Into command for inserting the records in a table.

```
Insert Into employee values(1,'Jagdish', 'CSE', 11, '2013-06-15',
'1976-01-11', 1101);
Insert Into employee values(2,'Alex', 'CSE', 11, '2013-06-15',
'1972-04-13', 1101);
Insert Into employee values(3,'Mohit', 'CSE', 11, '2013-07-11',
'1981-01-10', 1101);
Insert Into employee values(4,'Piyush', 'CSE', 11, '2015-06-14',
'1986-04-11', 1101);
Insert Into employee values(5,'Vivek', 'CSE', 11, '2016-06-12',
'1989-05-05', 1101);
Insert Into employee values(6,'Kriti', 'CSE', 11, '2018-06-01',
'1996-05-11', 1101);
Insert Into employee values(7,'Manisha', 'CSE', 11, '2019-09-15',
'1966-01-11', 1101);
Insert Into employee values(8,'Parisha', 'CSE', 11, '2021-08-13',
'1999-01-11', 1101);
```

Output Shown in the table 2.9
8 Records Inserted

```
Select * from employee; (will be used to retrieve all the records from
employee table)
```

Output:

TABLE 2.9

Employee Table

Empid	Empname	Dept	Deptid	DOJ	DOB	Dept No
1	Jagdish	CSE	11	2013-06-15	1976-01-11	1101
2	Alex	CSE	11	2013-06-15	1972-04-13	1101
3	Mohit	CSE	11	2013-07-11	1981-01-10	1101
4	Piyush	CSE	11	2015-06-14	1986-04-11	1101
5	Vivek	CSE	11	2016-06-12	1989-05-05	1101
6	Kriti	CSE	11	2018-06-01	1996-05-11	1101
7	Manisha	CSE	11	2019-09-15	1966-01-11	1101
8	Parisha	CSE	11	2021-08-13	1999-01-11	1101

Question: Delete the record of that employee whose empid is 6.
Answer: Here, we will use the delete command for deleting record whose empid is 6.

```
Delete from employee where empid=6;
```

Output Shown in the table 2.10
1 record deleted

*Select * from employee; (will display the complete set of records after deletion)*

TABLE 2.10

Employee Table after Deletion

Empid	Empname	Dept	Deptid	DOJ	DOB	Dept No
1	Jagdish	CSE	11	2013-06-15	1976-01-11	1101
2	Alex	CSE	11	2013-06-15	1972-04-13	1101
3	Mohit	CSE	11	2013-07-11	1981-01-10	1101
4	Piyush	CSE	11	2015-06-14	1986-04-11	1101
5	Vivek	CSE	11	2016-06-12	1989-05-05	1101
7	Manisha	CSE	11	2019-09-15	1966-01-11	1101
8	Parisha	CSE	11	2021-08-13	1999-01-11	1101

Note: While deleting from a table, we have to make sure to use unique value in condition, otherwise multiple records can be affected.

In the above example, we want to delete a record, but if we use dept, the records will be deleted because all the records have the same value for dept.

Question: Change the value of name by Parisha Patni of the employee whose empid is 8.
Answer: We will use the update command here for updating the value of name whose empid is 8.

Update employee
Set name='Parisha Patni' where empid=8;

Output Shown in the table 2.11
1 Record Updated

*Select * from employee;*

TABLE 2.11

Employee Table after Updating

Empid	Empname	Dept	Deptid	DOJ	DOB	Dept No
1	Jagdish	CSE	11	2013-06-15	1976-01-11	1101
2	Alex	CSE	11	2013-06-15	1972-04-13	1101
3	Mohit	CSE	11	2013-07-11	1981-01-10	1101
4	Piyush	CSE	11	2015-06-14	1986-04-11	1101
5	Vivek	CSE	11	2016-06-12	1989-05-05	1101
7	Manisha	CSE	11	2019-09-15	1966-01-11	1101
8	Parisha Patni	CSE	11	2021-08-13	1999-01-11	1101

Note: Here, the value of empname is updated by Parisha Patni, but make sure that you use unique values to make the appropriate changes, otherwise the changes may affect other records as well.

In case we use dept value in the where clause, then all the records will be updated as dept having the same values for all the records.

Update employee

```
Set name='Parisha Patni' where dept='CSE';
```

The above query will result in changes in all the records

```
Select* from employee; (will result in the table 2.12.)
```

TABLE 2.12

Employee Table after Updating Dept

Empid	Empname	Dept	Deptid	DOJ	DOB	Dept No
1	Parisha Patni	CSE	11	2013-06-15	1976-01-11	1101
2	Parisha Patni	CSE	11	2013-06-15	1972-04-13	1101
3	Parisha Patni	CSE	11	2013-07-11	1981-01-10	1101
4	Parisha Patni	CSE	11	2015-06-14	1986-04-11	1101
5	Parisha Patni	CSE	11	2016-06-12	1989-05-05	1101
7	Parisha Patni	CSE	11	2019-09-15	1966-01-11	1101
8	Parisha Patni	CSE	11	2021-08-13	1999-01-11	1101

2.7 Summary

It is crucial to understand the important commands in SQL to understand the basics of using and manipulating the dataset. The commands help us in various functions, including writing, updating, modifying, and deleting the data from the tables.

A database system provides a DDL to specify the database schema and DML to express database queries and updates. In practice, the DDL and DML are not two separate languages; instead, they simply form parts of a single database language, such as the widely used SQL language. We specify a database schema by a set of definitions expressed by a special language called DDL. DCL is used to manage roles, permissions, and referential integrity on the database. TCL manages the issues and matters related to the transactions in any database. They are used to rollback or commit the changes in the database.

References

1. Patni, J.C., Sharma, H.K., Tomar, R., & Katal, A. (2022). *Database Management System: An Evolutionary Approach* (1st ed.). Chapman and Hall/CRC. https://doi.org/10.1201/9780429282843
2. Risch, T. (2009). Query Language. In: Liu, L., Özsu, M.T. (Eds.) *Encyclopedia of Database Systems*. Springer, Boston, MA. https://doi.org/10.1007/978-0-387-39940-9_1090

3. 'Database Languages', [online]. Available: https://studyexperts.in/blog/database/database-language-in-dbms/, [Accessed: 12 April 2022].
4. 'Programming Languages and Compilers for Database Application Development', [online]. Available: https://www.ibm.com/docs/en/db2/10.5?topic=software-programming-languages-compilers, [Accessed: 12 April 2022].
5. Watt, Adrienne, & Eng, Nelson, 'SQL Structured Query Language', [online]. Available: https://opentextbc.ca/dbdesign01/chapter/sql-structured-query-language/, [Accessed: 12 May 2022].
6. 'What Is the Relational Database Management System', [online]. Available: https://www.codecademy.com/article/what-is-rdbms-sql, [Accessed: 12 May 2022].
7. 'An Introduction to SQL Commands', [online]. Available: https://www.simplilearn.com/tutorials/sql-tutorial/sql-commands, [Accessed: 12 December 2021].

3

Data and Integrity Constraints

In database management systems (DBMS), integrity constraints are a predefined set of rules that are applied to the table fields (columns) or relations to ensure that the overall validity, integrity, and consistency of the data in the database table is maintained. Evaluation of all the conditions or rules mentioned in the integrity constraint is done every time a table insert, update, delete, or alter operation is performed. The data can be inserted, updated, deleted, or altered only if the result of the constraint comes out to be true. Thus, integrity constraints are useful in preventing any accidental damage to the database by an authorized user.

Data integrity is having correct and accurate data in our database. When we are storing data in the database, we don't want repeating values; we don't want incorrect values or broken relationships between tables. So, let's understand through an example how broken relationships can cause data inconsistency.

3.1 Introduction

Data integrity can be maintained using constraints. These constraints define the rules according to which the operations like updation, deletion, insertions, etc., have to be performed to maintain the data integrity. There are mainly four types of data integrity:

1. Domain integrity
2. Entity integrity
3. Referential integrity
4. User-defined integrity

3.1.1 Domain Integrity

Domain refers to the range of acceptable values. It refers to the range of values we will accept and store in a particular column within a database. The data types available are mainly integer, text, date, etc. Any entry that we make for a column should be available in the domain of the data type.

```
Create table employee
(
Empid varchar(10),
Empname varchar(10),
Dept varchar(10),
```

DOI: 10.1201/9781003324690-3

```
Deptid integer,
City char(10),
DOJ Date,
DOB Date
);
```

In the above table, the domains of all the attributes are defined, which means that attributes will accept only defined values. For example, deptid is defined as an integer, so it will only accept the integer values as inserted in table 3.1.

TABLE 3.1

Employee Table

Empid	Empname	Dept	Deptid	DOJ	DOB	Dept No
1	Jagdish	CSE	11	2013-06-15	1976-01-11	1101
2	Alex	CSE	11	2013-06-15	1972-04-13	1101
3	Mohit	CSE	11	2013-07-11	1981-01-10	1101
4	Piyush	CSE	11	2015-06-14	1986-04-11	1101
5	Vivek	CSE	11	2016-06-12	1989-05-05	1101
6	Kriti	CSE	11	2018-06-01	1996-05-11	1101
7	Manisha	CSE	11	2019-09-15	1966-01-11	1101
8	Parisha	CSE	11	2021-08-13	1999-01-11	1101
9	Jatin	CSE	11A	2021-08-13	1999-01-11	1101

As we can only insert the integer values for the deptid, it means that record no 9 is wrong, and we can't insert this record.

3.1.2 Entity Integrity

Each row for an entity in a table should be uniquely identified. The entity constraint says that the value of the attribute can't be null as it is used for uniquely identifying. If the value of the attribute is NULL, then we can't uniquely identify the rows if all other fields are the same.

```
Create table employee
(
Empid varchar(10),
Empname varchar(10),
Dept varchar(10),
Deptid integer,
City char(10),
DOJ Date,
DOB Date
);
```

In the above table, empid can uniquely identify the records as every employee will have a unique id. We will discuss the concept in detail in the next section.

3.1.3 Referential Integrity

Referential integrity is used to maintain the data consistency between two tables. Rules are made in the database structure about how the foreign keys should be used to ensure that changes, addition, and deletion in the database maintain the data integrity. The referential integrity constraints state that if a foreign key in the first table refers to the primary key of the second table, then every value of foreign key in the first table should either be null or present in the second table.

```
Create table branch
(
Branchname varchar(10),
Branchcity varchar(10)
);

Create table account
(
Accountno number,
Branchname varchar(10),
Balance integer
);
```

In the above tables, the branch acts as the parent table and the account acts as child table. Here while entering the values in the account table, it will ensure that the value of the branch name should exist in the branch table; then the only record will be inserted, otherwise the record will be rejected. This concept where we refer to the values from one relation to the another is called referential integrity. The complete details about this will be discussed in the following section of the foreign key.

3.1.4 User-Defined Integrity

Sometimes this three integrity, i.e., domain, referential, and entity integrity, are not enough to maintain the data integrity. Such integrity is typically implemented through triggers and stored procedures. Triggers are a block of statements that executes automatically if any predefined events occur.

> *Example 1:* Whenever any new row is inserted into a student_table that has marks of different subjects of students, then automatically new average is calculated and stored.
> We can also define some user-defined constraints and specific business rules here.
> *Example 2:* We are creating a table for registration and want the user's age to be greater than 21. Such type of constraint is set by the user.

The DBMS keys represent one or more attributes (depending on the types of the DBMS keys used) from any table in the database system that brings about to distinctively categorize a row and/or a combination of more than one column, to identify the relationship between the tuple (row) in the table, or to determine the relationship between the two tables, which applies to the

3.2 Types of Keys in DBMS

The various types of keys used in DBMS are:

1. Super key
2. Candidate key
3. Primary key
4. Alternate key
5. Foreign key
6. Compound key
7. Surrogate key

3.2.1 Super Key

Super key is either a single key or a set of keys that help identify distinct rows in a particular table. A super key can have extra attributes that are redundant for distinct identification.

Let us look at an example where the Empid and the mobile number can be considered the super keys.

```
Create table employee
(
Empid varchar(10),
Empname varchar(10),
Dept varchar(10),
Deptid integer,
City char(10),
DOJ Date,
DOB Date
);
```

In the above table, multiple super keys are possible like empid, (Empid,empname), (empid, dept), (empid, city), etc.

3.2.2 Candidate Key

We can use a minimal super key uniquely identifying the records from a relation called a candidate key. A super key will suffer from complexity as the number of attributes are part of key; it will increase the complexity, so our is aim to reduce the size of key.

Let us look at an example of a table where the Empid, mobile no, and email can individually and uniquely identify the records from a relation so all three attributes will be the candidate's keys for the relation.

```
Create table employee
(
Empid varchar(10),
Empname varchar(10),
```

```
Mobileno integer,
Dept varchar(10),
Deptid integer,
City char(10),
Emailid varchar(20),
DOJ Date,
DOB Date
);
```

3.2.3 Primary Key

A relation will have multiple candidate keys, and any one of the candidate keys can act as the primary key in relation to uniquely identify the records. A primary key can have one or more attributes, but only one primary key is allowed in a relation. A primary key will ensure that no two records will have the same value for the primary key attributes.

If an attribute or set of attributes is defined as the primary key, then it will ensure that

- A primary key cannot be NULL>
- No duplicate values for any two rows under the primary key attribute.

```
Create table employee
(
Empid varchar(10) Primary Key,
Empname varchar(10),
Dept varchar(10),
Deptid integer,
City char(10),
DOJ Date,
DOB Date
);
```

TABLE 3.2

Employee Table with Primary Key

Empid	Empname	Dept	Deptid	DOJ	DOB	Dept No
1	Parisha	CSE	11	2013-06-15	1976-01-11	1101
2	Anustha	CSE	11	2013-06-15	1972-04-13	1101
3	Anurag	CSE	11	2013-07-11	1981-01-10	1101
4	Amit	CSE	11	2015-06-14	1986-04-11	1101
5	Bhavesh	CSE	11	2016-06-12	1989-05-05	1101
7	Rohit	CSE	11	2019-09-15	1966-01-11	1101
8	Shrey	CSE	11	2021-08-13	1999-01-11	1101

In the above table 3.2, empid is the primary key, so it has unique values for empid.

Primary key will be declared by the method where we can declare in front of the attribute, but if more than one attributes are part of the primary key, then this method will not work. In such cases, we will declare by the following method.

```
Create table employee
(
Empid varchar(10),
Empname varchar(10),
Dept varchar(10),
Deptid integer,
City char(10),
DOJ Date,
DOB Date,
Primary Key (Empid, deptid)
);
```

TABLE 3.3

Employee Table with Combination of Two Attributes as Primary Key

Empid	Empname	Dept	Deptid	DOJ	DOB	Dept No
1	Parisha	CSE	11	2013-06-15	1976-01-11	1101
1	Parisha	CSE	12	2013-06-15	1972-04-13	1101
2	Anustha	CSE	11	2013-07-11	1981-01-10	1101
3	Anurag	CSE	11	2015-06-14	1986-04-11	1101
3	Anurag	CSE	12	2016-06-12	1989-05-05	1101
4	Amit	CSE	11	2019-09-15	1966-01-11	1101
4	Amit	CSE	12	2021-08-13	1999-01-11	1101

In the above table 3.3, the combination of empid and deptid is unique. Primary key will ensure that no two rows have the same value for the attribute declared as the primary key.

If the primary key was not declared while the declaration of the table, then by the alter command, we can add the same in later stages.

```
Crate table emp
(
Empid varchar(10),
Name varchar(10),
City char(10),
Salary number(10,2)
);
```

In the above table, no primary key was declared, so we can add the following command

```
Alter Table emp add primary key (empid);
```

If we want to drop the primary key in later stages, then we can use the drop command to do the same.

```
Alter table emp drop primary key;
```

3.2.4 Alternate Key

A table may have more than one option for a key being selected as the primary key. Any key capable of being the primary key, but at the moment is not the primary key is known as an alternate key. It is a candidate key that has not been selected as the primary key.

Let us look at an example where the Empid, email, and the mobile no. are candidate keys and capable of being the primary key. But because Empid is the primary key, so email and mobile no. become the alternate key.

```
Create table employee
(
Empid varchar(10) Primary Key,
Empname varchar(10),
Mobileno integer,
Dept varchar(10),
Deptid integer,
City char(10),
Emailid varchar(20),
DOJ Date,
DOB Date
);
```

3.2.5 Foreign Key

Foreign key helps us in establishing relationships with other tables. It is also called referential integrity. A foreign key column can be added to a table to establish this relationship. They help us in maintaining data integrity and allow easy navigation between any instances of two entities.

Let us look at an example comprising of two tables, account, and branch table.

```
Create table branch
(
Branchname varchar(10) Primary Key,
Branchcity varchar(10)
);
```

```
Create table account
(
Accountno number Primary Key,
Branchname varchar(10) references branch,
Balance integer
);
```

Alternatively, we can write the table by the following syntax.

```
Create table account
(
Accountno number Primary Key,
```

```
Branchname varchar(10),
Balance integer,
Foreign Key (branchname)   references branch
);
```

Note: If the foreign key of the child relation and primary key of the parent relation have the same name, then we need not provide the attribute name while referring; otherwise, we have to mention the attribute name in the reference.

Example

```
Create table branch
(
Branchname varchar(10) Primary Key,
Branchcity varchar(10)
);

Create table account
(
Accountno number Primary Key,
Bname varchar(10) references branch (branchname),
Balance integer
);
```

Bname in account table acts as foreign key, which refers the attribute branchname in the branch table.

In above the table's branch and account, we can see that branch acts as parent table and the account serves as the child table. Account table will have a foreign key branchname that refers the values to the branch table to check whether the values are present in the branch table or not; if the values are present in the branch table, then only record will be allowed to enter into the account table that can be verified by table 3.4 and table 3.5.

TABLE 3.4

Branch (parent)

Branchname	branchcity
Bidholi	Dehardun
Rajnagar	Ghaziabad
Nakote	Pithoragarh
Jhajra	Dehradun

TABLE 3.5

Account

Accountno	Branchname	Balance
101	Bidholi	1000
102	Rajnagar	5000
103	Nakote	10000
104	Premnagar	2000

The record having account no. value 104 will not be added in the account relation because it will not find the Premnagar branch in the branch relation, so the record will be rejected with an error parent key not found.

We can add and remove the foreign key constraints in later stages with the following alter commands

```
Alter table account add foreign key (branchname) references branch
(branchname);
Alter table emp drop foreign key;
```

3.3 Check Constraints

The check constraint is an integrity constraint that controls the value in a particular column. It ensures inserted or updated value in a column must be matched with the given condition. In other words, it determines whether the value associated with the column is valid or not with the given condition.

For example, we have to create an employee table and ensure that empid start with E.

The syntax for the above query will be

```
Create table employee
(
Empid varchar(10) Primary Key,
Empname varchar(10),
Dept varchar(10),
Deptid integer,
City char(10),
DOJ Date,
DOB Date,
Check (empid like 'E%')
);
```

In the above create table syntax, we have added the check constraint that will ensure that all the values of empid star with E, otherwise the record will be rejected.

Let us understand with the help of the following examples.

```
Insert Into employee values('1','Jagdish', 'CSE', 11, '2013-06-15',
'1976-01-11', 1101);
```

In the above insert into, the roll no value is 1, but as per the check constraint, the value should start with E, so the record is rejected.

Once we start with E, then the record will be inserted into the relation.

```
Insert Into employee values('E1','Jagdish', 'CSE', 11, '2013-06-15',
'1976-01-11', 1101);
Insert Into employee values('E2','Alex', 'CSE', 11, '2013-06-15',
'1972-04-13', 1101);
```

```
Insert Into employee values('E3','Mohit', 'CSE', 11, '2013-07-11',
'1981-01-10', 1101);
Insert Into employee values('E4','Piyush', 'CSE', 11, '2015-06-14',
'1986-04-11', 1101);
Insert Into employee values('E5','Vivek', 'CSE', 11, '2016-06-12',
'1989-05-05', 1101);
Insert Into employee values('E6','Kriti', 'CSE', 11, '2018-06-01',
'1996-05-11', 1101);
Insert Into employee values('E7','Manisha', 'CSE', 11, '2019-09-15',
'1966-01-11', 1101);
Insert Into employee values('E8','Parisha', 'CSE', 11, '2021-08-13',
'1999-01-11', 1101);
```

Output of the above queries will be in table 3.6

TABLE 3.6

Employee Table with Check Constraints

Empid	Empname	Dept	Deptid	DOJ	DOB	Dept No
E1	Jagdish	CSE	11	2013-06-15	1976-01-11	1101
E2	Alex	CSE	11	2013-06-15	1972-04-13	1101
E3	Mohit	CSE	11	2013-07-11	1981-01-10	1101
E4	Piyush	CSE	11	2015-06-14	1986-04-11	1101
E5	Vivek	CSE	11	2016-06-12	1989-05-05	1101
E6	Kriti	CSE	11	2018-06-01	1996-05-11	1101
E7	Manisha	CSE	11	2019-09-15	1966-01-11	1101
E8	Parisha	CSE	11	2021-08-13	1999-01-11	1101

We can use multiple check constraints in a table for performing multiple conditions.

3.4 Unique Constraints

The UNIQUE constraint prevents two records from having identical values in a column. In the CUSTOMERS table, for example, you might want to prevent two or more people from having an identical age.

Example   For example, the following SQL query creates a new table called student. Here, the mobile column is set to UNIQUE, so we cannot have two records with the same mobile number.

```
Create table student
(
Rollno varchar(10) Primary Key,
Name char(10),
```

```
City char(10),
Age int,
Mobile integer NOT NULL unique
);
```

If the student table has already been created, add a UNIQUE constraint to the mobile column. We can write a statement like a query given in the code block below.
Alter table student

```
Modify mobile integer not null unique;
```

Similarly, we can drop the UNIQUE constraint by the following command
Alter table student

3.5 Domain Constraints

A domain of possible values should be associated with every attribute. These domain constraints are the most basic form of integrity constraint.
They are easy to test for when data is entered.

Domain types

Domains of an attribute may be null or not null, depending on its characteristics.
NULL: The attribute value can be null, depending on the following cases

1. Value is not available
2. Value is unknown
3. Value is missed
4. Value may be incorrect

In all the above cases, we can mark it as NULL, so the attribute property should be defined under NULL.

Example

```
Create table student
(
Rollno varchar(10) Primary Key,
Name char(10),
City char(10),
Age int,
Mobile integer NOT NULL unique
);

Insert into student values ('A101', 'Jatin', "NULL", 32, 67889765);
```

In the above example, the name and city attributes are not defined as not null, so by default, they are null, so we can enter the value NULL if any of the cases appears as defined above.

NOT NULL: If the values are mandatory and we can't leave them NULL, then we have to specify NOT NULL in the attribute property while declaring.

Example

```
Create table student
(
Rollno varchar(10) Primary Key,
Name char(10),
City char(10),
Age int,
Mobile integer NOT NULL unique
);

Insert into student values ('A101', 'Jatin', "NULL", 32, 67889765);
```

In the above example, mobile number is NOT NULL, so have to mandatory give the value of a mobile number.

3.6 Summary

SQL constraints are a set of rules implemented on tables in relational databases to dictate what data can be inserted, updated, or deleted in its tables. This is done to ensure the accuracy and the reliability of information stored in the table. Constraints enforce limits to the data or type of data that can be inserted/updated/deleted from a table. The purpose of constraints is to maintain the data integrity during an update/delete/insert into a table. Once the constraint is placed, if any operation in the database does not follow the rules specified by the constraint, the particular operation is aborted. Many types of constraints are discussed above, like primary key, foreign key, check, domain constraints, etc., to ensure the integrity of the database.

References

1. Patni, J.C., Sharma, H.K., Tomar, R., & Katal, A. (2022). *Database Management System: An Evolutionary Approach* (1st ed.). Chapman and Hall/CRC. https://doi.org/10.1201/9780429282843
2. 'Understanding SQL Constraints', [online]. Available: https://www.digitalocean.com/community/conceptual_articles/understanding-sql-constraints, [Accessed: 27 December 2021].
3. 'Constraints Clause', [online]. Available: https://docs.oracle.com/javadb/10.8.3.0/ref/rrefsqlj13590.html, [Accessed: 22 December 2021].

4. 'SQL CHECK Constraint', [online]. Available: http://www-db.deis.unibo.it/courses/TW/ DOCS/w3schools/sql/sql_check.asp.html, [Accessed: 13 December 2021].
5. 'SQL Constraints', [online]. Available: https://www.journaldev.com/28821/sql-constraints, [Accessed: 23 December 2021].
6. 'SQL Constraints', [online]. Available: https://www.linkedin.com/pulse/sql-constraints-umesh-rathod/?trk=articles_directory, [Accessed: 01 December 2021].
7. 'Table Constraints', [online]. Available: https://www.oreilly.com/library/view/oracle-sqlplus-the/0596007469/ch10s04.html, [Accessed: 08 December 2021].
8. 'Managing Constraints', [online]. Available: https://sqldatabasetutorials.com/sql-db/managing-constraints/, [Accessed: 03 December 2021].

4

Query Execution and Aggregate Functions

The query execution component applies the physical plan generated by the query optimizer. That plan should ensure a minimal memory footprint and I/O operations, as well as a fast execution time.

4.1 Select Statement

The SQL SELECT statement is used to fetch the data from a relation stirred inthe database, which returns this data as a result table. These result tables are called result sets.

4.1.1 Single Attribute Selection

It selects the single attribute from an existing table/relation.

Syntax Select attribute name from table name;

TABLE 4.1

Employee

Empid	Empname	Dept	Deptid	DOJ	DOB	DeptNo
E1	Jagdish	CSE	11	2013-06-15	1976-01-11	1101
E2	Alex	CSE	11	2013-06-15	1972-04-13	1101
E3	Mohit	CSE	11	2013-07-11	1981-01-10	1101
E4	Piyush	CSE	11	2015-06-14	1986-04-11	1101
E5	Vivek	CSE	11	2016-06-12	1989-05-05	1101
E6	Kriti	CSE	11	2018-06-01	1996-05-11	1101
E7	Manisha	CSE	11	2019-09-15	1966-01-11	1101
E8	Parisha	CSE	11	2021-08-13	1999-01-11	1101

Example: Find out the names of all the employees from the above employee table 4.1.

Query: Select empname from employee;

DOI: 10.1201/9781003324690-4

Output: The above query will find all the names from the employee table and results shown in table 4.2.

TABLE 4.2

Single Attribute Select Operation on Empname

Empname
Jagdish
Alex
Mohit
Piyush
Vivek
Kriti
Manisha
Parisha

Example: Find out the empid of all the employees from the above employee table.

Query: Select empid from employee;

Output: The above query will find all the empid's from employee table and results shown in table 4.3.

TABLE 4.3

Single Attribute Select Operation on Empid

Empid
E1
E2
E3
E4
E5
E6
E7
E8

4.1.2 Multiple Attribute Selection

This select method selects the multiple attributes from a relation/table.

Syntax

```
Select attribute1, attribute2..........., attributeN from table name;
```

Example: Find out the empid's and names of all the employees from the above employee table.

Query: Select empid, empname from employee;

Output: The above query will find all the empids and names from employee table and results shown in table 4.4.

TABLE 4.4

Multiple Attribute Select Operation 1

Empid	Empname
E1	Jagdish
E2	Alex
E3	Mohit
E4	Piyush
E5	Vivek
E6	Kriti
E7	Manisha
E8	Parisha

Example: Find out the empids, names, date of joining, and date of birth of all the employees from the above employee table.

Query: Select empid, empname, DOJ, DOB from employee;

Output: The above query will find all the emp ids, names, date of joining, and date of birth from the employee table and results shown in table 4.5.

TABLE 4.5

Multiple Attribute Select Operation 2

Empid	Empname	DOJ	DOB
E1	Jagdish	2013-06-15	1976-01-11
E2	Alex	2013-06-15	1972-04-13
E3	Mohit	2013-07-11	1981-01-10
E4	Piyush	2015-06-14	1986-04-11
E5	Vivek	2016-06-12	1989-05-05
E6	Kriti	2018-06-01	1996-05-11
E7	Manisha	2019-09-15	1966-01-11
E8	Parisha	2021-08-13	1999-01-11

4.1.3 Complete Table Selection

This select command is used once we want to fetch the complete table from the database.

Syntax

Select * from Table name;

Example: Find out all the records from the employee table.

*Query: Select * from employee*

Output: Will display all the records from the employee table and results shown in table 4.6.

TABLE 4.6

Complete Table Select Operation

Empid	Empname	Dept	Deptid	DOJ	DOB	DeptNo
E1	Jagdish	CSE	11	2013-06-15	1976-01-11	1101
E2	Alex	CSE	11	2013-06-15	1972-04-13	1101
E3	Mohit	CSE	11	2013-07-11	1981-01-10	1101
E4	Piyush	CSE	11	2015-06-14	1986-04-11	1101
E5	Vivek	CSE	11	2016-06-12	1989-05-05	1101
E6	Kriti	CSE	11	2018-06-01	1996-05-11	1101
E7	Manisha	CSE	11	2019-09-15	1966-01-11	1101
E8	Parisha	CSE	11	2021-08-13	1999-01-11	1101

4.1.4 Distinct Selection

This is used to select the distinct values of selected attribute during distinct selection.

If more than one row has the same values for the selected attributed, then only distinct values will only be extracted as results as shown in table 4.7, or we can say that duplicate values will be eliminated.

Syntax   Select distinct attribute name from table name;

TABLE 4.7

Complete Table Select Operation with Distinct

Empid	Empname	Dept	Deptid	DOJ	DOB	DeptNo
E1	Jagdish	CSE	11	2013-06-15	1976-01-11	1101
E2	Alex	CSE	11	2013-06-15	1972-04-13	1101
E3	Alex	CSE	11	2013-07-11	1981-01-10	1101
E4	Piyush	CSE	11	2015-06-14	1986-04-11	1101
E5	Vivek	CSE	11	2016-06-12	1989-05-05	1101
E6	Vivek	CSE	11	2018-06-01	1996-05-11	1101
E7	Parisha	CSE	11	2019-09-15	1966-01-11	1101
E8	Parisha	CSE	11	2021-08-13	1999-01-11	1101

Example: Find the distinct names of employees from the emp table.

Select distinct empname from EMP;

Output: Will display the distinct values of employee names and the results shown in table 4.8.

TABLE 4.8

Single Attribute Select Operation with Distinct Name

Empname
Jagdish
Alex
Piyush
Vivek
Parisha

Example: Select distinct values of the department from emp table.

Query: Select distinct dept from EMP;

Output: As shown in the table 4.9.

TABLE 4.9

Single Attribute Select Operation with Distinct Dept

Dept
CSE

4.1.5 Where Clause

Where clause is always used with select statement to fulfil the condition. Using where clause, we can display the output as per given predicate/condition.

Syntax

Select attribute1, attribute2, …….., attributeN from table name where [condition];

TABLE 4.10

Employee Table for Where Clause

Empid	Empname	Dept	Deptid	DOJ	DOB	DeptNo
E1	Jagdish	CSE	11	2013-06-15	1976-01-11	1101
E2	Alex	CSE	11	2013-06-15	1972-04-13	1101
E3	Mohit	CSE	11	2013-07-11	1981-01-10	1101
E4	Piyush	CSE	11	2015-06-14	1986-04-11	1101
E5	Vivek	CSE	11	2016-06-12	1989-05-05	1101
E6	Kriti	CSE	11	2018-06-01	1996-05-11	1101
E7	Manisha	CSE	11	2019-09-15	1966-01-11	1101
E8	Parisha	CSE	11	2021-08-13	1999-01-11	1101

Example: Find out the names of employees table 4.10 born after 11 November 1976.

Query: Select empname from emp where DOB> '1976-01-11';

Output: will display the names of all those employees who born after 11 November 1976 and the results shown in the table 4.11.

TABLE 4.11

Single Attribute Selection with Where Clause

Empname
Mohit
Piyush
Vivek
Kriti
Manisha
Parisha

Example: Find out the names of all the employees whose date of joining is 15 June 2013.

Query: Select empname from emp where DOJ= '2013-06-15';

Output: Will display the names of employees shown in the table 4.12 who joined on 15 June 2013 by putting the condition in where clause.

TABLE 4.12

Single Attribute Selection with Where Clause on DOJ

Empname
Jagdish
Alex

4.2 Aggregate Functions

An aggregate function in SQL performs a calculation on multiple values and returns a single value. SQL provides many aggregate functions, including avg, count, sum, min, max, etc. An aggregate function ignores NULL values when it performs the calculation, except for the count function.

An aggregate function in SQL returns one value after calculating multiple values of a column. We often use aggregate functions with the GROUP BY and HAVING clauses of the SELECT statement.

Various types of SQL aggregate functions are:

- Count()
- Sum()
- Avg()
- Min()
- Max()

4.2.1 Average

This function calculates the average from a set of values based on the attributes.

Syntax

Select avg(attribute name) from table name;

Creating a table employee with the following details

```
Create table employee
(
Empid integer Primary Key,
Name varchar(20) Not null,
```

```
City char(10) not null,
Salary number (10,2) not null,
Deptname char(10) not null,
Deptid integer not null,
Check (salary !=0)
);
```

Inserting the records in the above-created employee table.

```
Insert into employee values (101,'Amit', 'Dehradun','80000', 'CSE',01);
Insert into employee values (102,'Arun', 'Dehradun','80000', 'CSE',01);
Insert into employee values (131,'Bhavesh', 'Mumbai','90000', 'ECE',02);
Insert into employee values (104,'Charu', 'Haridwar','70000', 'CSE',01);
Insert into employee values (105,'Deepak', 'Roorkee','70000', 'ECE',02);
Insert into employee values (106,'Gaurav', 'Pithoragarh','50000',
'CSE',01);
Insert into employee values (107,'Hitesh', 'Tehri','70000', 'ME',03);
Insert into employee values (108,'Jagdish', 'Pauri','40000', 'CSE',01);
Insert into employee values (109,'Parisha', 'Nainital','80000', 'ME',03);
Insert into employee values (110,'Priyanka', 'Haldwani','85000',
'ECE',02);
Insert into employee values (111,'Shrey', 'Haldwani','87000', 'CSE',01);
```

Retrieve the above-inserted records by select command.

*Select * from employee;*

Output: Table 4.13 is the output after executing the above query.

TABLE 4.13

Employee Table for Aggregate Functions

Empid	Name	City	Salary	Deptname	Deptid
101	Amit	Dehradun	80000	CSE	01
102	Arun	Dehradun	80000	CSE	01
103	Bhavesh	Mumbai	90000	ECE	02
104	Charu	Haridwar	70000	CSE	01
105	Deepak	Roorkee	70000	ECE	02
106	Gaurav	Pithoragarh	50000	CSE	01
107	Hitesh	Tehri	70000	ME	03
108	Jagdish	Pauri	40000	CSE	01
109	Parisha	Nainital	80000	ME	03
110	Priyanka	Haldwani	85000	ECE	02
111	Shrey	Haldwani	87000	CSE	01

Question: Find out the average salary from the above employee table.

Query: Select avg(salary) from employee;

Output:

72909

In the above result, we will get the value of the average salary, but no column name is mentioned as the average salary column is not present in the employee table.

If we want to add a name from the desired output, we have to add a comment like below.

Query: Select avg(salary)"Average" from employee;

Output: Table 4.14 shows the average salary from the employee table.

TABLE 4.14

Select Average

Average
72909

4.2.2 Count()

This aggregate function returns the number of rows from a table.

Syntax

Select count(*) from table name;

This will display the total number of rows from a table.

Question: Find out the total number of rows from the employee table.

Query: Select count(*) from employee

Output:

11

Again if we want to give the name of the output, then we have to mention it in the comment.

Query: Select count(*) "Total Number of Rows" from employee;

Output: Table 4.15 shows the total number of records in the employee table.

TABLE 4.15

Select Number of Rows

Total Number of Rows
11

If we want the total number of values for the individual attribute, then we have to mention it in the count function.

Query: Select count(deptname) from employee;

Output: Table 4.16 shows the total number of dept. name in the employee table.

TABLE 4.16

Select Number of Rows Based on Attribute

Dept name
11

4.2.3 Sum()

Sum function is used to calculate the sum of any attribute values.

Syntax

Select Sum(attribute name) from table name;

Question: Find the sum of salaries from the employee table.

Query: select sum (salary) from employee;

Output:

802000

Select sum (salary)"Total cost" from employee;

Output: Table 4.17 shows the sum of cost from the employee table.

TABLE 4.17

Select Sum

Total cost
802000

4.2.4 Min()

This function is used to find out the minimum value from the selected attribute.

Syntax

Select min (attribute name) from table name;

Question: Find out the minimum salary from the employee table.

Query: Select min (salary) from employee;

Output: Table 4.18 shows the minimum salary from the employee table.

40000

Query: Select min (salary) "Minimum" from employee;

TABLE 4.18

Select Minimum Salary

Minimum
40000

4.2.5 Max()

This function is used to determine the maximum value from the selected attribute.

Syntax

Select max (attribute name) from table name;

Question: Find out the maximum salary from the employee table.

Query: Select max (salary) from employee;

Output: Table 4.19 shows the maximum salary from the employee salary.

90000

Query: Select max (salary) "Maximum" from employee;

TABLE 4.19

Select Maximum Salary

Maximum
40000

4.3 Order By Clause

This command is used to organize the records in specific orders. It may be either in ascending or descending order of the values of an attribute.

Syntax

Select * from Table name order by attribute name

This will display the records in the ascending order of the given attribute as shown in the table 4.20 where records are in the ascending order of name.

Example: Find out the records in the ascending order of name;

*Query: Select * from employee order by name;*

TABLE 4.20

Select Using Order By

Empid	Name	City	Salary	Deptname	Deptid
101	Amit	Dehradun	80000	CSE	01
102	Arun	Dehradun	80000	CSE	01
103	Bhavesh	Mumbai	90000	ECE	02
104	Charu	Haridwar	70000	CSE	01
105	Deepak	Roorkee	70000	ECE	02
106	Gaurav	Pithoragarh	50000	CSE	01
107	Hitesh	Tehri	70000	ME	03
108	Jagdish	Pauri	40000	CSE	01
109	Parisha	Nainital	80000	ME	03
110	Priyanka	Haldwani	85000	ECE	02
111	Shrey	Haldwani	87000	CSE	01

Example: Find out the records in the ascending order of salary.

Query: select from employee order by salary;*

Output: Here we can see that all the records are in the increasing order of salary as shown in table 4.21 from the employee table.

TABLE 4.21

Select Using Order By on Salary

Empid	Name	City	Salary	Deptname	Deptid
108	Jagdish	Pauri	40000	CSE	01
106	Gaurav	Pithoragarh	50000	CSE	01
104	Charu	Haridwar	70000	CSE	01
105	Deepak	Roorkee	70000	ECE	02
107	Hitesh	Tehri	70000	ME	03
109	Parisha	Nainital	80000	ME	03
101	Amit	Dehradun	80000	CSE	01
102	Arun	Dehradun	80000	CSE	01
110	Priyanka	Haldwani	85000	ECE	02
111	Shrey	Haldwani	87000	CSE	01
103	Bhavesh	Mumbai	90000	ECE	02

Example: Find out the names of employees from the employee table in the ascending order of salary;

Query: Select name form employee order by salary;

Output: Shown in the table 4.22.

TABLE 4.22

Select Name Using Order By of Salary

Name
Jagdish
Gaurav
Charu
Deepak
Hitesh
Parisha
Amit
Arun
Priyanka
Shrey
Bhavesh

Let's display the records in descending order. In such case, we will use the following syntax.

Select * from table name order by attribute name desc;

Desc is used to organize the records in the descending order of the selected attribute.

Example: Find out the records from the employee table in the descending order of salary.

*Query: Select * from employee order by salary desc;*

Output: Shown in the table 4.23.

TABLE 4.23

Select Employee Descending Order of Salary

Empid	Name	City	Salary	Deptname	Deptid
103	Bhavesh	Mumbai	90000	ECE	02
111	Shrey	Haldwani	87000	CSE	01
110	Priyanka	Haldwani	85000	ECE	02
102	Arun	Dehradun	80000	CSE	01
101	Amit	Dehradun	80000	CSE	01
109	Parisha	Nainital	80000	ME	03
107	Hitesh	Tehri	70000	ME	03
105	Deepak	Roorkee	70000	ECE	02
104	Charu	Haridwar	70000	CSE	01
106	Gaurav	Pithoragarh	50000	CSE	01
108	Jagdish	Pauri	40000	CSE	01

Example: Find out the names of employees from the employee table in the descending order of salary;

Query: Select name form employee order by salary desc;

Output: Shown in the table 4.24.

TABLE 4.24

Select Name from Employee Descending of Salary

Name
Bhavesh
Shrey
Priyanka
Arun
Amit
Parisha
Hitesh
Deepak
Charu
Gaurav
Jagdish

4.4 Group By Clause

The GROUP BY clause is used with the SELECT statement to show the common data of the column from the table:

Syntax of SELECT Statement with GROUP BY clause

SELECT column_Name_1, column_Name_2, ..., column_Name_N aggregate_function_name(column_Name2) FROM table_name GROUP BY column_Name1;

Example: Find out the total number of employees department-wise.

In this example, we have to find out the total number of employees in each department, so here, we will use the GROUP BY command on the deptname that will calculate the total number of employees per the unique value of deptname.

Query: Select deptname, Count(*)"Total Employees" from employee group by deptname;

Output: Shown in the table 4.25.

TABLE 4.25

Select Using Group By

Deptname	Total Employees
CSE	06
ECE	03
ME	02

Example: Find out the average salary department-wise.

In this example, we have to find the average salary department-wise, so it will calculate the average of all those records having the same values of deptname.

Query: Select deptname, avg(salary) "Average"from employee group by deptname;

Output: Shown in the table 4.26.

TABLE 4.26

Select Using Group By to Calculate Average Department-wise

Deptname	Average
CSE	67833
ECE	81667
ME	75000

4.5 Having Clause

This is a conditional statement that will be used with the GROUP BY command. Having clause is used to check for a given predicate.

Syntax

SELECT column_Name_1, column_Name_2, ..., column_Name_N aggregate_function_name(column_Name2) FROM table_name GROUP BY column_Name1 having [condition];

Example: Find out the total number of employees department-wise having more than two employees.
In this example, we have to find out the total number of employees in each department with more than two employees. In this statement, we will use the having predicate to check the condition. The output is shown in the table 4.27.

Query: Select deptname, Count(*)" Total Employees" from employee group by deptname having count(deptname)>2;

TABLE 4.27

Select Using Having Clause 1

Deptname	Total Employees
CSE	06
ECE	03

Example: Find out the average salary department-wise having more than 75000.
In this example, we have to find the average salary department-wise having more than average salary of 75,000.

Query: Select deptname, avg(salary) "Average"from employee group by deptname having avg (salary)>75000;

Output: Shown in the table 4.28.

TABLE 4.28

Select Using Having Clause 2

Deptname	Average
ECE	81667

4.6 Examples

1. Find out the name of that employee whose salary is maximum.

   Query: Select name from employee where salary= (select max (salary) from employee);
   The above query will compare the salary with the maximum salary and get the name of that employee.

   Output: Shown in the table 4.29.

   TABLE 4.29

   Example 1

Name
Bhavesh

2. Find out the name of that employee whose salary is minimum.

   Query: Select name from employee where salary= (select min (salary) from employee);
   The above query will compare the salary with the minimum salary and get the name of that employee.

   Output: Shown in the table 4.30.

   TABLE 4.30

   Example 2

Name
Jagdish

3. Find out the second maximum salary from employee table.

   Query: Select max(salary) from employee where salary< (select max (salary) from employee);
   The above query will exclude the maximum salary from the relation and then find the maximum salary from rest of the records.

Output: Shown in the table 4.31.

TABLE 4.31

Example 3

87000

4. Find out the name of the second highest paid employee.

Query: Select name from employee where salary= (Select max(salary) from employee where salary< (select max (salary) from employee));
The above query will exclude the maximum salary from the relation and then find the maximum salary record from the rest of the records. Finally, get the name of that employee

Output: Shown in the table 4.32.

TABLE 4.32

Example 4

Name

Shrey

5. Find out the name of all those employees whose salary is greater than average salary.
Query: Select name from employee where salary> (select avg(salary) from employee);
The above query will compare the salary with the average salary and get the names of all those employees whose salary is greater than average.

Output: Shown in the table 4.33.

TABLE 4.33

Example 5

Name

Amit
Arun
Bhavesh
Parisha
Priyanka
Shrey

4.7 Summary

An aggregate function performs a calculation of one or more values and returns a single value. The aggregate function is often used with the GROUP BY clause and HAVING clause of the SELECT statement. The SQL order of execution defines the order in which the clauses of a query are evaluated. Some of the most common query challenges are easily avoided with a clearer understanding of the SQL order of execution, sometimes called the SQL order of operations. Understanding SQL query order can help you diagnose why a query won't run and, even more frequently, will help you optimize your queries to run faster.

References

1. Olivier Cure, & Guillaume Blin, (2015). Query Processing, *RDF Database Systems*, Morgan Kaufmann, 145–167, ISBN 9780127999579, https://doi.org/10.1016/B978-0-12-799957-9.00006-7
2. 'SQL Server Aggregate Functions', [online]. Available: https://www.sqlservertutorial.net/sql-server-aggregate-functions/, [Accessed: 12 January 2022].
3. Patni, J.C., Sharma, H.K., Tomar, R., & Katal, A. (2022). *Database Management System: An Evolutionary Approach* (1st ed.). Chapman and Hall/CRC. https://doi.org/10.1201/9780429282843
4. 'Aggregate Function', [online]. Available: https://docs.microsoft.com/en-us/sql/t-sql/functions/aggregate-functions-transact-sql?view=sql-server-ver15, [Accessed: 12 January 2022].
5. 'Aggregate Functions', [online]. Available: https://www.ibm.com/docs/en/db2-for-zos/11?topic=functions-aggregate, [Accessed: 25 January 2022].
6. 'Aggregate Function Descriptions', [online]. Available: https://dev.mysql.com/doc/refman/8.0/en/aggregate-functions.html, [Accessed: 18 January 2022].
7. 'Aggregate Functions', [online]. Available: https://docs.oracle.com/database/121/SQLRF/functions003.htm#SQLRF20035, [Accessed: 17 January 2022].
8. 'SQL Query Order of Execution', [online]. Available: https://www.sisense.com/blog/sql-query-order-of-operations/, [Accessed: 11 January 2022].
9. 'Query Processing Architecture Guide', [online]. Available: https://docs.microsoft.com/en-us/sql/relational-databases/query-processing-architecture-guide?view=sql-server-ver15, [Accessed: 16 January 2022].

5

SQL Server vs. Oracle

5.1 Design Schema

Oracle is a RDBMS designed to minimize errors in the physical database systems. It can run on various operating systems like Linux, UNIX, Windows, and many more. It comes with cross-platform features, and it is also the first RDBMS system developed and dedicated to manipulating records of business-based databases.

Key Features of Oracle

Oracle is equipped with a range of features to counter the need of users, which gives it an edge compared to other databases. Some of them are:

- It can operate on a large amount of data too quicker.
- It provides a higher degree of scalability, portability, distribution, and programmability.
- It is the first RDBMS that was made for business purposes.
- It is a cross-platform database that can run on 60+ platforms, from mainframes to Apple Macs.
- It is designed to be used on several operating systems such as **z/OS, Linux, UNIX, OS X**, and **Windows**.
- It provides data reliability and integrity services, following the atomicity, consistency, isolation, and durability (ACID) properties.
- In Oracle, communication between different platforms is easy, which is supported by many networking stacks.
- Its recovery manager tool manages database backups and assists in database recoveries.
- Oracle is written in assembly language, C, and C++.
- It supports Extensible Markup Language (XML).
- It also supports both SQL and PL/SQL language.

SQL Server

SQL Server, developed in 1989 by Microsoft, is also an RDBMS. Like other traditional RDBMSs, like MySQL and PostgreSQL, SQL Server also utilizes SQL to manage data in its

DOI: 10.1201/9781003324690-5

database. SQL is a declarative query processing language that provides users access to data on SQL Server easily and efficiently.

Key Features of SQL Server

SQL Server has some distinctive features that make it an admired database in the current market scenario. Some of them are:

- It supports multiple tools, such as SQL Server Management Studio, Database Tuning Advisor, SQL Server Profiler, and BI.
- It comes with 24×7 online help and support capabilities.
- It supports high-level programming languages like Java and Python.
- For an application that uses SQL, it is suited for backend programming.
- It improves the query optimizer output and makes it much more efficient with the intelligent query processing enhancements built into it.

SQL Server is simple in use due to the similarity of syntax to SQL. Database sharing is not an option for users. Packages are not in use here, and its software processing power is lower than Oracle.

Design schema is bagged with the definitions of the tables, views, indexes, users, constraints, stored procedures, triggers, and other database-specific objects required for relational databases work. These objects are mostly similar to other RDBMS.

5.1.1 Similarities between SQL Server and Oracle

Both Oracle and Microsoft SQL Server share many similar schema objects but still differ in a small set of schema objects, as shown in the following Tables 5.1–5.3:

5.1.2 Schema Object Names

There are reserved words for schema object names, which differ in each Oracle and Microsoft SQL Server. In Oracle, DATE is a reserved word, but not in Microsoft SQL Server, and that's why no column in Oracle can be assigned the name DATE while in Microsoft SQL Server, it can be assigned. Therefore, reserved words used for schema object names can't be used to name across databases.

For both Oracle and Microsoft SQL Server naming schema object names, we need to choose that word that is either unique by the case or at least by one other characteristic from the reserved word.

5.1.3 Design Issues

This section discusses the many table design issues we need to consider when converting Microsoft SQL Server databases to Oracle as shown in the table 5.1. The issues will be covered by the following topics:

- Data Types
- Entity Integrity Constraints

TABLE 5.1

Schema Objects in Oracle and Microsoft SQL Server

Oracle	SQL Server
Database	Database
Schema	Database and database owner (DBO)
Tablespace	Database
User	User
Role	Group/role
Table	Table
Column-level check constraint	Column-level check constraint
Primary key	Primary key
Foreign key	Foreign key
Index	Nonunique index
PL/SQL procedure	Transact-SQL (T-SQL) stored procedure
PL/SQL function	T-SQL stored procedure
Packages	NA
AFTER triggers	TRIGGERS
BEFORE triggers	Complex rules
Triggers for each row	NA
Sequences	Identity property for a column
Snapshot	NA
View	View

- Referential Integrity Constraints
- Unique Key Constraints
- Check Constraints

5.1.3.1 Data Types

This section describes conversion considerations for the following data types:

DATETIME Data Types
IMAGE and TEXT Data Types (Binary Large Objects)
Microsoft SQL Server User-Defined Data Types

DATETIME Data Types

The date/time precision in Microsoft SQL Server is 1/300th of a second. Oracle has the data type TIMESTAMP, which has a precision of 1/100000000th of a second. Oracle also has a DATE data type that stores date and time values accurate to one second. SQL Developer has a default mapping to the DATE data type.

When there is a requirement for more accurate date/time precision than seconds in Microsoft SQL Server, then TIMESTAMP data type is chosen for the data type mapping. The databases store point-in-time values for DATE and TIME data types.

Also, if Microsoft SQL Server uses DATETIME column to give unique IDs rather than point-in-time values, we can use SEQUENCE instead of DATETIME column in the Oracle schema definition.

In the below example, DATETIME precision was originally designed such that it does not allow it to exceed seconds in the Oracle tab. This example assumes that the DATETIME column is used to provide unique IDs. The following example's table design outlined is satisfactory if the user does not require millisecond precision:

Microsoft SQL Server

```
Create table table_name
(
Attribute_name datetime not Null,
Attribute_name text Null,
Attribute_name varchar(10) Not Null
);
```

Oracle

```
Create table table_name
(
Attribute_name date not Null,
Attribute_name long Null,
Attribute_name varchar2(10) Not Null
);
```

For inserting the value of the sequence into the integer_column, following table design can be used. This gives us the power to order the rows in the table beyond the allowed precision of one second for DATE data type fields in Oracle. If we add this column to the Microsoft SQL Server table, we can have the same table design for the Oracle database.

Revised Table Design

Microsoft SQL Server

```
Create table table_name
(
Attribute_name datetime not Null,
Attribute_name integer Null,
Attribute_name text Null,
Attribute_name varchar(10) Not Null
);
```

Oracle

```
Create table table_name
(
Attribute_name date not Null,
Attribute_name long Null,
Attribute_name number Null,
```

```
Attribute_name varchar2(10) Not Null
);
```

For the Microsoft SQL Server database, the value in the integer_column is always NULL. For Oracle, the value for the field integer_column is updated with the next value of the sequence.

Create the sequence by issuing the following command:

```
Create Sequence Sequence_name
Start with 1
Increment by 1
Max value 100
No cycle;
```

Values generated for this sequence start at 1 and are incremented by 1.

IMAGE and TEXT Data Types (Binary Large Objects)

There is a difference in physical and logical storage methods for IMAGE and TEXT data, from Oracle to Microsoft SQL Server. A pointer in Microsoft SQL Server for IMAGE or TEXT data is kept in rows in the table while the IMAGE or TEXT data are stored separately. This gives us the flexibility of having multiple columns of IMAGE or TEXT data per table. In Oracle, IMAGE data may be stored in a BLOB type field, and TEXT data may be stored in a CLOB type field. Oracle can facilitate multiple BLOB and CLOB columns per table. BLOBS and CLOBS may or may not be stored in the row, depending on their size.

Microsoft SQL Server User-Defined Data Types Microsoft SQL Server T-SQL-specific enhancement to SQL has allowed users to define and name their own data types along with already existing system data types. A user-defined data type is allowed to be used as the data type for any column in the database. Defaults and rules (check constraints) can be included with these user-defined data types, which will be applied repeatedly to each column under these user-defined data types.

When migrating to Oracle PL/SQL, the Migration Workbench finds the base data type for each user-defined data type and determines the equivalent PL/SQL data type.

5.1.3.2 Entity Integrity Constraints

We can define a primary key for a table in Microsoft SQL Server. Primary keys can be defined in a CREATE TABLE or ALTER TABLE statement.

A primary key can be defined as part of a CREATE TABLE or ALTER TABLE statements. Oracle internally creates a unique index to enforce integrity.

5.1.3.3 Referential Integrity Constraints

We can define a foreign key for a table in Microsoft SQL Server. Foreign key can be defined in a CREATE TABLE or ALTER TABLE statements.

Oracle provides declarative referential integrity. A CREATE TABLE or ALTER TABLE statements can add foreign keys to the table definition.

5.1.3.4 Unique Key Constraints

We can define a unique key for a table in Microsoft SQL Server. Unique keys can be defined in a CREATE TABLE or ALTER TABLE statements.

Oracle defines unique keys as part of CREATE TABLE or ALTER TABLE statements. Oracle internally creates unique indexes to enforce these constraints.

Unique keys map one-to-one from Microsoft SQL Server to Oracle.

5.1.3.5 Check Constraints

Check constraints can be defined in a CREATE TABLE or ALTER TABLE statements in Microsoft SQL Server. Multiple check constraints can be defined on a table. A table-level check constraint can reference any column in the constrained table. A column can have only one check constraint. A column-level check constraint can reference only the constrained column. These check constraints support complex regular expressions.

Oracle defines check constraints as part of the CREATE TABLE or ALTER TABLE statements. A check constraint is defined at the TABLE level and not at the COLUMN level. Therefore, it can reference any column in the table. Oracle, however, does not support complex regular expressions.

5.2 Data Types

This provides detailed descriptions of the differences in data types as per table 5.2, used by Microsoft SQL Server and Oracle databases.

- The table shows the base Microsoft SQL Server data types available and how they are mapped to Oracle data types
- Recommendations based on the information listed in the table

TABLE 5.2

Data Types in Oracle and Microsoft SQL Server

Microsoft SQL Server	Description	Oracle
INTEGER	Four-byte integer, 31 bits, and a sign. abbreviated as "INT"	NUMBER(10)
SMALLINT	Two-byte integer, 15 bits, and a sign.	NUMBER(6)
TINYINT	One-byte integer, 8 bits, and no sign. Holds whole numbers between 0 and 255.	NUMBER(3)
REAL	Floating point number. Storage is four bytes and has a binary precision of 24 bits, a 7-digit precision. Data can range from −3.40E+38 to 3.40E+38.	FLOAT
FLOAT	A floating point number. This column has 15-digit precision.	FLOAT
BIT	A Boolean 0 or 1 is stored as one bit of a byte. Up to 8-bit columns from a table may be stored in a single byte, even if not contiguous. Bit data cannot be NULL.	NUMBER(1)
CHAR(n)	Fixed-length string of exactly n 8-bit characters, blank padded. Synonym for CHARACTER.	CHAR(n)

(Continued)

TABLE 5.2   (CONTINUED)

Data Types in Oracle and Microsoft SQL Server

Microsoft SQL Server	Description	Oracle
VARCHAR(n)	Varying-length character string.	VARCHAR2(n)
TEXT	Character string of 8-bit bytes allocated in increments of 2k pages. "TEXT" is stored as a linked list of 2024-byte pages, blank padded. TEXT columns can hold up to (231-1) character.	CLOB
IMAGE	Binary string of 8-bit bytes. Holds up to (231-1) bytes of binary data.	BLOB
BINARY(n)	Fixed-length binary string of exactly n 8-bit bytes. 0 < n < 256 for Microsoft SQL Server. 0 < n < 8000 for Microsoft SQL Server 7.0.	RAW(n)/BLOB
VARBINARY(n)	Varying length binary string of up to n 8-bit bytes. 0 < n < 256 for Microsoft SQL Server. 0 < n < 8000 for Microsoft SQL Server 7.0.	RAW(n)/BLOB
DATETIME	Date and time are stored as two 4-byte integers. The date portion is represented a count of the number of days offset from a baseline date (1/1/1900) and stored in the first integer.	DATE
SMALL-DATETIME	Date and time are stored as two 2-byte integers. Date ranges from 1/1/1900 to 6/6/2079. Time is the count of the number of minutes since midnight.	DATE
NCHAR(n)	Fixed-length character data type, which uses the UNICODE UCS-2 character set. n must be a value in the range 1 to 4000. SQL Server storage size is two times n.	CHAR(n*2)
NVARCHAR(n)	Fixed-length character data type, which uses the UNICODE UCS-2 character set. n must be a value in the range 1 to 4000. SQL Server storage size is two times n.	VARCHAR(n*2)
TIMESTAMP	TIMESTAMP is defined as VARBINARY(8) with NULL allowed. Every time a row containing a TIMESTAMP column is updated or inserted, the TIMESTAMP column is automatically incremented by the system. A TIMESTAMP column may not be updated by users.	NUMBER
SYSNAME	VARCHAR(30) in Microsoft SQL Server.	VARCHAR2(30)

TEXT and IMAGE data types in Microsoft SQL Server follow these rules:

- The column of these data types cannot be indexed.
- The column cannot be a primary key.
- The column cannot be used in the GROUP BY, ORDER BY, HAVING, and DISTINCT clauses.
- IMAGE and TEXT data types can be referred to in the WHERE clause with the LIKE construct.
- IMAGE and TEXT data types can also be used with the SUBSTR and LENGTH functions.

In Microsoft SQL Server, those columns specified as variable-length data types can only store NULL values. When we create a column and specify it as NULL with a fixed-length data type, the column is automatically transformed to a system variable-length data type, as illustrated in table 5.3. These variable-length data types are reserved system data types, and users are barred from using them to create columns.

TABLE 5.3

Data Type Conversion for NULL Values

Fixed-Length Data Type	Variable-Length Data Type
CHAR	VARCHAR
NCHAR	NVARCHAR
BINARY	VARBINARY
DATETIME, SMALLDATETIME	DATETIMN
FLOAT	FLOATN
INT, SMALLINT, TINYINT	INTN
DECIMAL	DECIMALN
NUMERIC	NUMERICN
MONEY, SMALLMONEY	MONEYN

5.3 Data Storage

This section provides a detailed description of the conceptual differences in data storage for the Microsoft SQL Server and Oracle databases.

Specifically, it contains the following information:

- Table 5.4 comparing the data storage concepts of Microsoft SQL Server and Oracle databases
- Recommendations based on the information listed in the table

5.4 DML Statement from SQL Server vs. Oracle

This section uses table 5.4 to compare the syntax and description of data manipulation language (DML) elements in the Microsoft SQL Server and Oracle databases. Each table is followed by a recommendations section based on the information in the tables. The following topics are presented in this section:

- Connecting to the Database
- SELECT Statement
- SELECT with GROUP BY Statement
- INSERT Statement
- UPDATE Statement
- DELETE Statement
- Operators
  - Comparison Operators
  - Arithmetic Operators
  - String Operators
  - Set Operators
  - Bit Operators

TABLE 5.4

Data Storage Concepts in Oracle and Microsoft SQL Server

Microsoft SQL Server	Oracle
Database Devices: A database device is mapped to the specified physical disk files.	**Data Files:** Depending upon each tablespace, **N**(decided by the requirement) number of data files are created to store the data of all logical structures physically.
Page: Many pages constitute a database device. Each page contains a certain number of bytes.	**Data Block:** A data block size can be fixed to **N** number of bytes on the disk, which can be specified during the creation of database. A database uses and allocates the free database space in Oracle data blocks.
Extent: Eight pages make one extent. Space is allocated to all the databases in increments of one extent at a time.	**Extent:** An extent is a specific number of contiguous data blocks, obtained in a single allocation.
N/A	**Segments:** A segment is a set of extents allocated for a certain logical structure.
Segments: A segment is a name given to one or more database devices. Segment names are used in CREATE TABLE and CREATE INDEX constructs to place these objects on specific database devices. The following segments are created along with the database: • System segment stores the system tables. • Log segment Stores the transaction log. • Default segment all other database objects are stored on this segment unless specified otherwise. Segments are subsets of database devices.	**Tablespace:** A database is divided into logical storage units called tablespaces. A tablespace is used to group related logical structures together. A database typically has one system tablespace and one or more user tablespaces. **Tablespace Extent:** An extent is a specific number of contiguous data blocks within the same tablespace. **Tablespace Segments:** A segment is a set of extents allocated for a certain logical database object. All the segments assigned to one object must be in the same tablespace. The segments get the extents allocated to them as and when needed.
Log Devices: These are logical devices assigned to store the log. The database device to store the logs can be specified while creating the database.	**Redo Log Files:** Each database has a set of two or more redo log files. All changes made to the database are recorded in the redo log.
Database Devices: A database device contains the database objects. A logical device does not necessarily refer to any particular physical disk or file in the file system.	N/A
Dump Devices These are logical devices where database dump is stored. The DUMP DATABASE command is used to dump the database using the dump device.	N/A
N/A	**Control Files:** Each database has a control file. This file records the physical structure of the database.

- Built-In Functions
  - Character Functions
  - Date Functions
  - Mathematical Functions

- Locking Concepts and Data Concurrency Issues
  - Locking
  - Row-Level vs. Page-Level Locking
  - Read Consistency
- Logical Transaction Handling

5.4.1 Connecting to the Database

The statement illustrated in Table 5.5 connects a user to a database.

TABLE 5.5

Connecting to the Database in Oracle and Microsoft SQL Server

Microsoft SQL Server	Oracle
Syntax:	Syntax:
Use database_Name	Connect user_name and password
Description:	
A default database is assigned to each user. When the user logs on to the server, database is made available. When they want to switch to another database, a user executes the USE DATABASE_NAME command.	

5.4.2 SELECT Statement

The following statement retrieves rows from one or more tables or views.

Select * from table_name where [condition]

Microsoft SQL Server supports SELECT statements that do not have a FROM clause. This can be seen in the following example.

Select getdate();

Oracle does not support SELECTs without FROM clauses. However, Oracle provides the DUAL table, which always contains one row. Use the DUAL table to convert constructs such as the preceding one.

Select sysdate from dual;

SELECT INTO Statement

The Microsoft SQL Server SELECT INTO statement can insert rows into a table. This construct, which is part SELECT and part INSERT, is not supported by ANSI. Replace these statements with INSERT…SELECT statements in Oracle.

If the Microsoft SQL Server construct is similar to the following:

```
Select attribute1, attribute2,…, attributeN
INTO Target_table
From source_table
Where [condition]
```

We should convert it to the following for Oracle:

```
insert into target_table
Select attribute1, attribute2,…, attributeN
From source_table
Where [condition]
```

INSERT INTO Statement

The INSERT INTO statement is used in Oracle and SQL Server as follows:

```
          INSERT INTO table_name (column1, column2, column3, …)
                  VALUES (value1, value2, value3, …);
                               OR
                     INSERT INTO table_name
                  VALUES (value1, value2, value3, …);
```

Delete Statement

The delete statement is used to delete the records from a selected relation.

Delete from table_name where [condition]

Update Statement

The update statement will update the values within the records.

```
Update table_name
Set attribute_name= new value where [condition]
```

5.5 Microsoft SQL Server vs. Oracle: The Same but Different

- SQL Server can run on a limited platforms while Oracle has a wider range of platforms.
- SQL Server doesn't facilitate query optimization, whereas Oracle supports star query optimization.
- SQL Server can change values frequently before committing, whereas Oracle changes only after committing.
- SQL Server doesn't have a rollback option during the transaction process, whereas Oracle has that facility.

- SQL server offers "Schemas" within each user database where Oracle supports many "Schemas" with the instance.
- SQL Server supports to full, partial, and incremental backups, whereas Oracle provides database with full, file-level, incremental, and differential backups.
- SQL Server mainly uses only "after" triggers, while Oracle uses both "after" and "before" triggers.

5.6 Summary

MS SQL Server is popular among users due to its simplicity over Oracle Database. Oracle database is preferred for larger organizations where a larger database is required, whereas MS SQL Server is mostly preferred for enterprises since it is only compatible with Windows and Linux. Handling of a group of tasks execution is known as transaction control which varies vastly in both databases. Let's compare a situation where a set of records must be updated simultaneously by default. In that case, SQL Server acts by executing each command selectively, and that way, it gets exceedingly difficult to change if any errors are found along the command lines. Oracle acts on each new database connection as a new transaction. After that, databases are organized. MS SQL Server organizes all objects by database names, such as tables, views, and procedures.

References

1. Patni, J.C., Sharma, H.K., Tomar, R., & Katal, A. (2022). *Database Management System: An Evolutionary Approach* (1st ed.). Chapman and Hall/CRC. https://doi.org/10.1201/9780429282843
2. 'Oracle vs SQL Server: 10 Critical Differences', [online]. Available: https://hevodata.com/learn/oracle-vs-sql-server/, [Accessed: 12 Febuary 2022].
3. 'Microsoft SQL Server vs. Oracle: The Same, But Different?', [online]. Available: https://www.seguetech.com/microsoft-sql-server-vs-oracle-same-different/, [Accessed: 10 Febuary 2022].
4. Microsoft SQL Server and Oracle Compared, 'Database SQL Developer Supplementary Information for Microsoft SQL Server Migrations', [online]. Available: https://docs.oracle.com/cd/E10405_01/appdev.120/e10379/ss_oracle_compared.htm, [Accessed: 21 Febuary 2022].
5. Olivia, 'Database Differences: Microsoft SQL Server vs. Oracle Database', [online]. Available: https://www.cybrary.it/blog/0p3n/database-differences-microsoft-sql-server-vs-oracle-database/, [Accessed: 28 Febuary 2022].
6. 'Microsoft SQL Server vs. Oracle Database', [online]. Available: http://dba-oracle.com/s_microsoft_sql_server_vs_oracle_database.htm, [Accessed: 23 March 2022].
7. 'SQL Server vs Oracle Terminology', [online]. Available: http://www.dba-oracle.com/t_sql_server_vs_oracle_terminology.htm, [Accessed: 23 March 2022].
8. 'Oracle Database Administration for Microsoft SQL Server DBAs', [online]. Available: https://www.oreilly.com/library/view/oracle-database-administration/9780071744317/, [Accessed: 20 Febuary 2022].

6

Conditional Statements and Operators in SQL

Conditional statements allow us to change the way our program behaves based on the input it receives, the contents of variables, or several other factors.

6.1 Introduction

A database encompasses one or multiple tables with rows and columns. Each table is represented by a name, and SQL statements are used to perform any action on a database. Here, we will discuss conditional statements in SQL, which are based on some conditional expressions. An expression can be any arrangement of SQL literals, like variables, operators, and functions that, on execution, returns a logical value if the condition is satisfied.

Although SQL isn't a general-purpose language, it includes conditional statements with a similar structure to other languages. The classic IF and CASE statements permit the ability to change data on the query level instead of modifying them in another environment, such as a worksheet or a data frame.

6.2 Conditional Evaluation

While neither of these statements is hard to master, especially with previous exposure to programming languages, they offer plenty of power and flexibility to modify query results. To demonstrate how these statements may be used, a simple table will be created detailing a student ID, name, department, and project.

```
Create table student
(
studentID Integer Primary Key,
name varchar (10),
department varchar(10),
project char(10)
);
```

DOI: 10.1201/9781003324690-6

6.3 Types of Condition

6.3.1 IF Condition

The most basic form of an IF statement in SQL looks very similar to conditional statements in most other programming languages and software.

If (condition, True, False) from table;

An IF statement simply introduces some condition and then returns a result based on whether the condition is true or false. When the condition is true, the second parameter is returned, and when false, the third parameter.

To give a more concrete example, suppose a student checks that either he achieved the goal or not based on the marks in the final examination.

Additionally, he don't want a filtered list of subjects in which he achieved the goal. He wants to check all the subjects from his course.

Select studentid, subject, if (marks>75, 'Achieved', 'Not Achieved') as goal from
    student;

The SELECT statement returns the studentID and subject as expected but also includes an IF statement. The first parameter introduces the condition of whether the marks are greater than 75. When the goal is achieved, the second parameter, "achieved" is returned and "Not achieved" when not achieved. To make the resulting query more readable, an alias is added to the IF statement, results are shown in the table 6.1.

TABLE 6.1

Select Using IF Condition

StudentID	Subject	Goal
101	Physics	Achieved
101	Chemistry	Not Achieved
101	Mathematics	Achieved
101	Information Technology	Achieved

Note: The above table represents the record of a student where student scores marks in different subjects. The query returned the values of studentID, subject, and goal achieved or not based on the conditions.

6.3.2 The CASE Statement

While the IF statement provides a basic conditional statement, it doesn't support multiple conditions. In that scenario, a CASE statement must be used.

```
Case field
When condition_1 then Statement_1
When condition_2 then Statement_2
Else Statement_3
End
From Table_name;
```

A CASE begins by specifying a field within the table. The WHEN…THEN statements create a specific condition and return statement. When *condition_1* is true, then *statement_1* is returned. The same applies for *condition_2 and statement_2*.

If none of the cases are fulfilled, an optional ELSE statement, sometimes referred to as the default case, returns *statement_3*. Note that the CASE statement must be closed with an END.

Suppose a student wants to check out the subject details and display subjects like Physics as PHY, Chemistry as CHEM, and Mathematics as MATHS.

Then, we will create a CASE statement for the same as follows.

```
Select StudentID, marks,
Case subject
When 'Physics' then 'PHY'
When 'Chemistry' then 'CHEM'
When 'mathematics' then 'MATHS'
END as 'Subject Code'
From student;
```

In the following WHEN…THEN clauses, the condition consequently also applies to the entry in the subject field. When the subject is equal to "Physics," then "PHY" is returned. The same applies to "Chemistry" and "CHEM" and "Mathematics" and "MATHS". END closes the CASE statement and includes an alias to make the results more readable results are shown in the table 6.2.

TABLE 6.2

Select Using CASE Condition

StudentID	Marks	Subject Code
101	73	PHY
101	78	CHEM
101	80	MATHS
102	83	PHY
102	67	CHEM
102	76	MATHS

As a result, the query returns a subject code instead of the subject name.

6.3.3 While Statement

The following flowchart explains the essential structure of the WHILE loop in SQL:

As you can see, in each iteration of the loop, the defined condition is checked, and then, according to the result of the condition, the code flow is determined. If the result of the condition is true, the SQL statement will be executed. Otherwise, the code flow will exit the loop. If any SQL statement exists outside the loop, it will be executed.

Syntax

```
While [condition]
Begin
Main Program
End Program
```

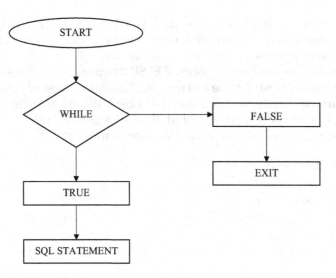

FIGURE 6.1
Flow chart of while condition.

In the example given below, the WHILE loop example will write a value of the variable ten times, and then the loop will be completed:

```
Declare
serialNo int=1
while(serialNo<=10)
Begin
Dbms_output.put_line(serialNo)
serialNo=serialNo+1
END
```

Output:

1
2
3
4
5
6
7
8
9
10

6.3.4 For Statement

A FOR LOOP is a repetition control structure that allows you to efficiently write a loop that needs to execute a specific number of times.

Syntax

```
For i in initial value .. final value LOOP
Statements
End Loop
```

Following is the flow of control in a FOR LOOP

The initial step is executed first and only once. This step allows you to declare and initialize any loop control variables.

Next, the condition, i.e., *initial_value .. final_value* is evaluated. If it is TRUE, the body of the loop is executed. If it is FALSE, the body of the loop does not execute and the flow of control jumps to the next statement just after the for loop.

After the body of the for loop executes, the value of the counter variable is increased or decreased.

The condition is now evaluated again. If it is TRUE, the loop executes, and the process repeats itself (body of loop, then increment step, and then again condition). After the condition becomes FALSE, the FOR LOOP terminates.

Following are some special characteristics of PL/SQL FOR -LOOP

- The *initial_value* and *final_value* of the loop variable can be literals, variables, or expressions but must evaluate to numbers. Otherwise, PL/SQL raises the predefined exception VALUE_ERROR.
- The *initial_value* need not be 1; however, the loop increment (or decrement) must be 1.
- SQL allows the determination of the loop range dynamically at run time.

Example

```
Declare
a number;
begin
for a in 1..10
LOOP
Dbms_output.put_line ('a:' ||a);
End Loop;
END;
/
```

When the above code is executed at the SQL prompt, it produces the following result:

a: 1

a: 2

a: 3

a: 4

a: 5

a: 6

a: 7

a: 8

a: 9

a: 10

Reverse FOR LOOP Statement

By default, iteration proceeds from the initial value to the final value, generally upward from the lower bound to the higher bound. You can reverse this order by using the REVERSE keyword. In such a case, iteration proceeds the other way. After each iteration, the loop counter is decremented.

However, you must write the range bounds in ascending (not descending) order. The following program illustrates this:

Example

```
Declare
a number;
begin
for a in Reverse 1..10
LOOP
Dbms_output.put_line ('a:' ||a);
End Loop;
END;
/
```

When the above code is executed at the SQL prompt, it produces the following result:

a: 10

a: 9

a: 8

a: 7

a: 6

a: 5

a: 4

a: 3

a: 2

a: 1

6.4 Operators

This section compares the different operators used in the Microsoft SQL Server and Oracle databases. It includes the following subsections:

- Arithmetic Operators
- Comparison Operators

- Logical Operators
- Negation Operator
- AND/OR operator

6.4.1 Arithmetic Operators

The arithmetic operators are used to perform mathematical operations on the numerical values stored in the database tables.

We can use these operators with the select statement with or without the condition.

We can use these operators between the two attribute having the similar domains.
The main arithmetic operators are as follows:

- ADD (+)
- SUSTRACT (-)
- MULTIPLY (*)
- DIVISION (/)
- MODULUS (%)

ADD Operator (+)

This operator performs the addition between the two or more attributes of similar domains.

Syntax

SELECT attribute_name1 + attribute_name2 from Table_Name;

Addition Operator with WHERE Clause
The addition operator can also be used with the WHERE clause

Syntax

SELECT attribute_name1 + attribute_name2 from Table_Name where [condition]

Let's take an example of the student as follows:

```
Create table Student
(
StudentID integer Primary Key,
Stuname char(10) Not Null,
Subject1marks integer not null,
Subject2marks integer not null,
Stucity varchar(10)
);
```

Let's insert the records in the above student table.

```
Insert into student values (101, 'Amit',80,71,'Lucknow');
Insert into student values (102, 'Shrey',83,72,'Dehradun');
```

```
Insert into student values (103, 'Parisha',81,75,'Delhi');
Insert into student values (104, 'Neha',83,78,'Haldwani');
Insert into student values (105, 'Pranav',83,79,'Kanpur');
Insert into student values (106, 'Rohit',85,77,'Gorakhpur');
```

Let's retrieve the records by executing the following query:

Select * from student;

Output: shown in the table 6.3.

TABLE 6.3

Student Table

StudentID	Stuname	Subject1marks	Subject2marks	stucity
101	Amit	80	71	Lucknow
102	Shrey	83	72	Dehradun
103	Parisha	81	75	Delhi
104	Neha	83	78	Haldwani
105	Pranav	83	79	Kanpur
106	Rohit	85	77	Gorakhpur

Example: Find the sum of both the subject marks from the student table.

Query: Select subject1marks+subject2marks as totalmarks from student;

The above query will add the marks for both the subjects and return the sum of them:

Output: shown in the table 6.4.

TABLE 6.4

Select Using ADD Operator 1

totalmarks
151
155
156
161
162
162

Example: Add the grace of 5 marks to each student in subject1marks.

Query: Select subject1marks+5 as FinalSubject1marks from student;

The above query will add the five additional marks to subject1marks for each student.

Output: shown in the table 6.5.

TABLE 6.5

Select Using ADD Operator 2

Finalsubject1marks
85
88

Finalsubject1marks
86
88
88
90

Example: Add the additional five marks to suject2marks for those students who have scored more than 80 marks in subject1marks.

Query: Select subject2marks+5 as FinalSubject2marks from student where subject1marks>80;

The above query will add the five additional marks to subject2marks only for those students who have scored more than 80 marks in subject1marks. In the results, we can see only five values of fianlsubject2marks will show as one of the students scored 80 marks in subject1marks, so it will not satisfy the condition.

Output: shown in the table 6.6.

TABLE 6.6

Select Using ADD Operator 2

Finalsubject2marks
77
80
83
84
82

Subtract Operator (-)

This operator will perform the subtraction between the values of two attributes of similar domains.

Syntax

SELECT attribute_name1 - attribute_name2 from Table_Name;

The subtraction operator can also be used with the WHERE clause

Syntax

SELECT attribute_name1 - attribute_name2 from Table_Name where [condition]

Refer to the above student table

Example: Find out the difference between the subject1marks and subject2marks from the student table.

Query: Query: Select subject1marks – subject2marks as difference from student;

The above query will get the difference between the two subjects and return the difference:

Output: shown in the table 6.7.

TABLE 6.7

Select Using Subtract Operator 1

Difference
9
9
6
5
4
8

Example: Find out the final marks for subject1marks for all subjects after deducting five marks as penalty.

Query: Select subject1marks – 5 as difference from student;

The above query will deduct the five marks from subject1marks as a penalty and print the marks after deduction. Results are shown in the table 6.8.

TABLE 6.8

Select Using Subtract Operator 2

Difference
75
78
76
78
78
80

Multiply Operator (*)

This operator will perform the multiplication between the values of two attributes of similar domains and do the multiplication with the defined value in query.

Syntax

SELECT attribute_name1* attribute_name2 from Table_Name;

The subtraction operator can also be used with the WHERE clause

Syntax

SELECT attribute_name1 * attribute_name2 from Table_Name where [condition]

Refer to the above student table
   Example: Final the subject1marks after multiplying by 1.10 factor.

*Query: Select subject1marks*1.10 as final marks from student;*

The above query will multiply the subject1marks by 1.10 factor and get the final result after rounding off the values.

Output: shown in the table 6.9.

TABLE 6.9

Select Using Multiply Operator

Final marks
88
91
89
91
91
95

Division Operator (/)

This operator will perform the division between the values of two attributes of similar domains and divide with the defined value in query.

Syntax

SELECT attribute_name1/ attribute_name2 from Table_Name;

The subtraction operator can also be used with the WHERE clause

Syntax

SELECT attribute_name1 / attribute_name2 from Table_Name where [condition]

Refer to the above student table
Example: Final the subject1marks after dividing by 1.10 factor.

Query: Select subject1marks/1.10 as final marks from student;

The above query will divide the subject1marks by 1.10 factor and get the final result after rounding off the values.

Output: shown in the table 6.10.

TABLE 6.10

Select Using Division Operator

Final marks
73
75
74
74
74
77

Modulus Operator (%)

The SQL Modulus Operator provides the remainder when the numerical values of one column are divided by the numerical values of another column.

Syntax

   SELECT attribute_name1% attribute_name2 from Table_Name;

The subtraction operator can also be used with the WHERE clause

Syntax

   SELECT attribute_name1 % attribute_name2 from Table_Name where [condition]

Refer to the above student table
   Example: Final the remainder after dividing subject1marks by subject2marks.

   Query: Select subject1marks %subject2marks as final marks from student;

   The above query will divide the subject1marks by subject2marks and display the reminder.

   Output: shown in the table 6.11.

TABLE 6.11

Select Using Modulus Operator

Final marks
9
11
6
5
4
8

6.4.2 Comparison Operator

A comparison operator is used to perform the comparison between the two different values of similar domains.
   These operators are used for making the comparison based on the condition given in the query. The query will display the records satisfying the condition as per the comparison operator.
   The following are the comparison operators used in SQL.

- Equal to (=)
- Greater than (>)
- Less than (<)
- Greater than equal to (>=)
- Less than equal to (<=)
- Not equal to (<>)

All the above comparison operators will work on similar kinds of attributes or domains.

Syntax

Select attribute_name1, attribute_name2 from table name where attribute_name[comparison operator] value;

Let's create an employee table

```
Create table employee
(
empID integer Primary Key,
name char(10) Not Null,
salary integer not null,
deptID integer not null,
city varchar(10)
);
```

Let's insert the records in the above student table.

```
Insert into employee values (101, 'Amit',80000,1,'Lucknow');
Insert into employee values (102, 'Shrey',83000,1,'Dehradun');
Insert into employee values (103, 'Parisha',81000,1,'Delhi');
Insert into employee values (104, 'Neha',83000,2,'Haldwani');
Insert into employee values (105, 'Pranav',83000,3,'Kanpur');
Insert into employee values (106, 'Rohit',85000,4,'Gorakhpur');
```

Let's retrieve the records by executing the following query:

*Select * from employee;*

Output: shown in the table 6.12.

TABLE 6.12

Employee Table

empID	name	Salary	deptID	city
101	Amit	80000	1	Lucknow
102	Shrey	83000	1	Dehradun
103	Parisha	81000	1	Delhi
104	Neha	83000	2	Haldwani
105	Pranav	83000	2	Kanpur
106	Rohit	85000	2	Gorakhpur

Equal to (=)

Example: Find out the names of all those employees whose salary is equal to 80,000.

Query: Select name from employee where salary=80000;

The above will return the names of all those employees whose salary equals 80,000 as we have used the equal to operator. Only one record is having 80000 salary, so Amit will come as output.

Output: shown in the table 6.13.

TABLE 6.13

Comparison Operator 1

name
Amit

Greater than (>)

Example: Find out the names of all those employees whose salary is greater than 82,000.

Query: Select name from employee where salary > 82000;

The above will return the names of all those employees whose salary is greater than 82,000 as we have used the greater than operator. Four records have more than 82,000 salary.

Output: shown in the table 6.14.

TABLE 6.14

Comparison Operator 2

name
Shrey
Neha
Pranav
Rohit

Less than (<)

Example: Find out the names of all those employees whose salary is less than 82,000.
Query: Select name from employee where salary < 82000;
The above will return the names of all those employees whose salary is less than 82,000 as we have used the less than operator. Two records is having less than 82,000 salary.

Output: shown in the table 6.15.

TABLE 6.15

Comparison Operator 3

name
Amit
Parisha

Greater than equal to (>=)

Example: Find out the names of all those employees whose salary is greater than or equal to 82000.

Query: Select name from employee where salary >= 82000;

The above will return the names of all those employees whose salary is greater than or equal to 82,000 as we have used the greater than or equal to operator. Four records will appear as output.

Output: shown in the table 6.16.

TABLE 6.16

Comparison Operator 4

name
Shrey
Neha
Pranav
Rohit

Less than equal to (<=)

Example: Find out the names of all those employees whose salary is less than or equal to 82,000.

Query: Select name from employee where salary <= 82000;

The above will return the names of all those employees whose salary is less than or equal to 82,000 as we have used the less than or equal to operator. Four records will appear as output.

Output: shown in the table 6.17.

TABLE 6.17

Comparison Operator 5

name
Amit
Parisha

Not equal to (<>)

Example: Find out the names of all those employees whose salary is not equal to 83,000.

Query: Select name from employee where salary <> 83000;

The above will return the names of all those employees whose salary is not equal to 83,000 as we have used the not equal to operator. Three records will appear as output.

Output: shown in the table 6.18.

TABLE 6.18

Comparison Operator 6

name
Amit
Parisha
Rohit

6.4.3 Logical Operators

The logical operators will return the result in one form, i.e., either it will display that the query is true or false. The results displayed to combine or merge more than one true or false data.

Logical operators are categorized as follows.

6.4.3.1 ANY Operator

The ANY operator is a logical operator that compares a value with a set of values returned by a subquery. The ANY operator must be preceded by a comparison operator >, >=, <, <=, =, <> and followed by a subquery.

Syntax

SELECT Attribute_name (s) FROM table_name WHERE attribute_name comparision
operator ANY(SELECT attribute_name FROM table_name WHERE [condition]);

Let's take an example of employee and department relation.

```
Create table employee
(
Empid varchar(10) Primary Key,
Empname char(10) Not Null,
deptID varchar(10) Not Null,
city char(10),
Project varchar(10)
);
```

```
Create table department
(
deptID varchar(10) Primary Key,
deptname char(10) not Null
);
```

Insert the records in the employee table.

```
Insert into employee values (101, 'Amit','E1','Lucknow', 'Marketing');
Insert into employee values (102, 'Shrey','E2','Dehradun', 'Finance');
Insert into employee values (103, 'Parisha','E2','Delhi', 'Finance');
Insert into employee values (104, 'Neha',"E1,'Haldwani', 'Marketing');
Insert into employee values (105, 'Pranav','E3','Kanpur', 'Sales');
Insert into employee values (106, 'Rohit','E3','Gorakhpur', 'Sales');
```

Retrieve the records by the following query.

Select* from employee;

Output: shown in the table 6.19.

TABLE 6.19

Employee Table

EmpID	Empname	DeptID	City	Project
101	Amit	E1	Lucknow	Marketing
102	Shrey	E2	Dehradun	Finance
103	Parisha	E2	Delhi	Finance
104	Neha	E1	Haldwani	Marketing
105	Pranav	E3	Kanpur	Sales
106	Rohit	E3	Gorakhpur	Sales

Insert the records in the department table.

```
Insert into department values ('E1', 'Customer Accounting');
Insert into department values ('E2', 'Customer Relation');
Insert into department values ('E3', 'Customer Management');
Insert into department values ('E4', 'Maintenance');
```

Retrieve the records by the following query

Select* from department;

Output: shown in the table 6.20.

TABLE 6.20

Department Table

DeptID	deptname
E1	Customer Accounting
E2	Customer Relation
E3	Customer Management
E4	Maintenance

Based on the above two relations, execute the following query.

Select project from employee where deptID = ANY (Select deptID from department);

The above query gives the list of projects running in any department in the department relation.

We can alternatively use this with where condition.

Select project from employee where deptID = ANY (Select deptID from department where deptname= 'customer Relation');

6.4.3.2 ALL Operator

The ALL operator returns a Boolean value as a result and returns TRUE if all subquery values meet the condition. The ALL operator can be used with the condition as well.

All means it should meet the conditions for all.

SELECT ALL Attribute_name(s) FROM table_name WHERE [condition];

SELECT Attribute_name (s) FROM table_name WHERE attribute_name comparison operator ALL (SELECT attribute_name FROM table_name WHERE [condition]);

Refer to the above table employee and department

Select ALL city from employee where true;

Will display all the city names from the employee relation.

Select project from employee where deptID = ALL (Select deptID from department where deptname= 'customer Relation');

The above SQL query lists all the project names if all the records in the department table have deptname is customer relation.

This will return False as all the department table records do not have the deptname as customer relation.

6.4.3.3 AND Operator

This operator is used to satisfy the multiple conditions in a single query.

Refer to the above employee table.

Example: Find out the names of all those employees whose city is Dehradun and the project is finance.

Query: Select empname from employee where city= 'Dehradun' and Project= 'Finance';

Output: This query will return the values if both the conditions are true, results are shown in table 6.21.

TABLE 6.21

Selection Using and Operator

Empname
Shrey

6.4.3.4 OR Operator

This operator is used to satisfy either of the conditions in a single query.

Refer to the above employee table.

Example: Find out the names of all those employees whose project name is either finance or sales.

Query: Select empname from employee where project= 'finance' or Project= 'Sales';

Output: This query will return the values for both the conditions, either the project name is finance or sales. Results are shown in table 6.22.

TABLE 6.22

Selection Using or Operator 1

Empname
Shrey
Parisha
Pranav
Rohit

Example: Find out the names of all those employees whose project name is finance or city is Kanpur.

Query: Select empname from employee where project= 'finance' or city= 'Kanpur';

Output: This query will return the values for both conditions, either the project name is finance or city equal to Kanpur. Results are shown in table 6.23.

TABLE 6.23

Selection Using OR Operator 2

Empname
Shrey
Parisha
Pranav

6.4.3.5 Between Operator

This operator is used to retrieve the records from a given range. Here, we have a start range and end range, so it will display the records between the given range in the query.

Refer to the above employee table.

Example: Find out the names of all those employees whose empID is between 102 and 105.

Query: Select empname from employee where empid between 102 and 105;

Output: This query will return the values of empnames where empid starting from 102 to 105. Results are shown in table 6.24.

TABLE 6.24

Selection Using Between Operator

Empname
Shrey
Parisha
Neha
Pranav

6.4.3.6 EXISTS Operator

The EXISTS operator is used to test for the existence of any record in a subquery. The EXISTS operator returns TRUE if the subquery returns one or more records.
Refer to the above employee and department table.

Query: Select empname from employee where exists (select deptID from department where deptname='Customer Relation');

Output: This query will return true and display the names of all those employees whose deptname is Customer Relation. Results are shown in table 6.25.

TABLE 6.25

Selection Using EXISTS Operator

Empname
Shrey
Parisha

6.4.3.7 IN Operator

IN operator is used to find the records from multiple values in condition. AND,OR operator is used to compare two values, but if we have to compare and retrieve from more than two values, then we will use the IN operator.
Refer to the above employee table
Example: Find out the names of all those employees whose cities are Delhi, Dehradun, Lucknow, or Haldwani.

Query: Select empname from employee where city in ('Delhi', 'Dehradun', 'Lucknow', 'Haldwani');

Output: This query will return true and display the names of all those employees whose city's names are given in query. Results are shown in the table 6.26.

TABLE 6.26

Selection Using IN Operator

Empname
Amit
Shrey
Parisha
Neha

6.4.3.8 LIKE Operator

The SQL LIKE operator compares a value to similar values using wildcard operators. There are two wildcards used with the LIKE operator.

Percent sign (%)

underscore (_)

The percent sign represents zero, one, or multiple characters. The underscore represents a single number or character. These symbols can be used in combinations.

Syntax

Select attribute_name(s) from table_name where attribute_name like '%A%';

This is used whether A character appears in the value irrespective of any place.

Select attribute_name(s) from table_name where attribute_name like 'A%';

This will ensure that the value should always start with A, and after that, any character can appear as per the domains of the attribute.

Select attribute_name(s) from table_name where attribute_name like '%A';

This will ensure that the value should always end with A, and before that, any character can appear as per the domains of the attribute.

Select attribute_name(s) from table_name where attribute_name like '_A%';

This will ensure that the second character will be A, and before that, any character can appear as well as after any number of characters can appear per the domains of the attribute.
Similarly, we can use of '_' to place the character at any position.
Refer to the above employee table.
Example: Find out the names of all those employees whose city's first character is L.

Query: select empname from employee where city like 'L%';

Output: This will display the names of all those employees whose city's names start with L. Results are shown in the table 6.27.

TABLE 6.27

Selection Using LIKE Operator 1

Empname
Amit

Example: Find out the names of all those employees whose city's last character is r.

Query: select empname from employee where city like '%r';

Output: This will display the names of all those employees whose city name end with r. Results are shown in the table 6.28.

TABLE 6.28

Selection Using LIKE Operator 2

Empname
Amit
Rohit

Example: Find out the names of all those employees whose city's second character is e.

Query: select empname from employee where city like '_e%';

Output: This will display the names of all those employees whose city second character is e irrespective of other characters. Results are shown in the table 6.29.

TABLE 6.29

Selection Using LIKE Operator 3

Empname
Shrey
Parisha

Example: Find out the names of all those employees whose city's name has a character 'a' in any place.

Query: select empname from employee where city like '%a%';

Output: This will display the names of all employees whose city has a character 'a' irrespective of any place. Results are shown in the table 6.30.

TABLE 6.30

Selection Using LIKE Operator 4

Empname
Amit
Shrey
Neha
Pranav
Rohit

6.4.3.9 NOT Operator

The SQL NOT condition is used to negate a condition in the WHERE clause of a SELECT, INSERT, UPDATE, or DELETE statement.

We will use the not (<>) symbol to use this operator, and this operator can also be used with IN operator.

Syntax

Select Attribute_name(s) from Table_name where attribute_name <> value
Refer to the above employee table.

Example: Find out the name of all those employees whose city is not in Lucknow.

Query: select empname from employee where city <> 'Lucknow';

Output: This will display the names of all those employees whose city is not in Lucknow. Results are shown in the table 6.31.

TABLE 6.31

Selection Using NOT Operator 1

Empname
Shrey
Parisha
Neha
Pranav
Rohit

Example: Find out the name of all those employees whose city is not in Lucknow, Delhi, and Dehradun.

Query: select empname from employee where city NOT IN ('Lucknow', 'Delhi', 'Dehradun');

Output: This will display the names of all those employees whose city is not in Lucknow, Delhi, and Dehradun. Results are shown in the table 6.32.

TABLE 6.32

Selection Using NOT Operator 2

Empname
Pranav
Rohit

6.4.3.10 IS NULL Operator

It is not possible to test for NULL values with comparison operators, such as =, <, or <>, so we use the IS NULL and IS NOT NULL to execute such kind of queries.

Syntax

Select Attribute_name(s) from Table_name where attribute_name IS NULL

Select Attribute_name(s) from Table_name where attribute_name IS NOT NULL

Refer to the above employee table.
    Example: Find out the names of all employees whose city IS NULL.

Query: select empname from employee where city IS NULL;

Output: This will not display any records as no city names are NULL.
NO record found
Example: Find out the name of all employees whose city IS NOT NULL.

Query: select empname from employee where city IS NOT NULL;

Output: This will display all the records as no city names are not NULL. Results are shown in the table 6.33.

TABLE 6.33

Selection Using NOT NULL Operator

Empname
Amit
Shrey
Parisha
Neha
Pranav
Rohit

6.4.3.11 UNIQUE Operator

This operator will display the unique values of attributes used with select statement.

Syntax:

Select unique Attribute_name(s) from Table_name where [condition]

Refer to the above employee table.
   Example: Find out the unique name of all those employees.

Query: select unique empname from employee;

Output: This will display all the empnames as all the values of names are unique in the table employee. Results are shown in the table 6.34.

TABLE 6.34

Selection Using UNIQUE Operator 1

Empname
Amit
Shrey
Parisha
Neha
Pranav
Rohit

Example: Find out the unique deptID from employee table.

Query: select unique deptID from employee;

Output: This will display unique deptID from employee table and eliminate the duplicates. Results are shown in the table 6.35.

TABLE 6.35

Selection Using UNIQUE Operator 2

DeptID
E1
E2
E3

6.5 Summary

Conditional statements define the logic to be executed based on the status of some condition being satisfied.

The SQL Else If statement is useful to check multiple conditions at once. SQL Else If statement is an extension to the If then.

If Else statement only executes the statements when the given condition is either true or false. But in the real world, we may have to check more than two conditions. In these situations, we can use the SQL Else If statement.

Different arithmetic and logical operators are used during selection to execute the specific set of queries to satisfy the given predicate.

References

1. Patni, J.C., Sharma, H.K., Tomar, R., & Katal, A. (2022). *Database Management System: An Evolutionary Approach* (1st ed.). Chapman and Hall/CRC. https://doi.org/10.1201/9780429282843
2. 'Conditional Statement in SQL', [online]. Available: https://www.ibm.com/docs/en/ias?topic=procedures-conditional-statements, [Accessed: 22 May 2022].
3. 'Creating Conditional Statement in SQL', [online]. Available: https://towardsdatascience.com/creating-conditional-statements-in-sql-queries-a25339c4f44d, [Accessed: 12 May 2022].
4. 'Conditional Statement in where Clause', [online]. Available: https://www.sqlservercentral.com/articles/conditional-statements-in-where-clauses, [Accessed: 15 May 2022].
5. Jason Andress, & Ryan Linn, Conditional Statement, Science Direct.2017.
6. 'PL/SQL If Statement', [online]. Available: https://www.oracletutorial.com/plsql-tutorial/plsql-if/, [Accessed: 05 May 2022].
7. 'Conditional and Sequential Control', [online]. Available: https://www.oreilly.com/library/view/oracle-plsql-programming/9781449324445/ch04.html, [Accessed: 01 May 2022].
8. 'Conditional Expressions', [online]. Available: https://teradata.github.io/presto/docs/0.167-t/functions/conditional.html, [Accessed: 07 May 2022].

7

Nested Query and Join

One of the challenges in writing SQL queries is choosing whether to use a subquery or a JOIN. There are many situations in which a JOIN is the better solution, and there are others where a subquery is better. Let's consider this topic in detail.

Subqueries are used in complex SQL queries. Usually, there is a main outer query and one or more subqueries nested within the outer query.

Subqueries can be simple or correlated. Simple subqueries do not rely on the columns in the outer query, whereas correlated subqueries refer to data from the outer query.

The JOIN clause does not contain additional queries. It connects two or more tables and selects data from them into a single result set. It is most frequently used to join tables with primary and foreign keys.

Subqueries and JOINs can be used in a complex query to select data from multiple tables, but they do so differently. Sometimes we have a choice of either, but there are cases in which a subquery is the only real option.

7.1 Understanding Subquery

A subquery is a SELECT statement coded within another SELECT statement. A subquery has two parts: the outer query and inner query, and an inner query again can have multiple queries based on the problem. A subquery will return a single value or multiple values based on the problem. A subquery can be used with select, insert, update, and delete commands.

Syntax

Select Attribute_name(s) from table where [condition] operator (Select Attribute_name(s) from table where [condition])

Refer to the following employee in table 7.1 and department table in table 7.2.

TABLE 7.1

Employee Table

EmpID	Empname	DeptID	City	Project
101	Amit	E1	Lucknow	Marketing
102	Shrey	E2	Dehradun	Finance
103	Parisha	E2	Delhi	Finance
104	Neha	E1	Haldwani	Marketing
105	Pranav	E3	Kanpur	Sales
106	Rohit	E3	Gorakhpur	Sales

DOI: 10.1201/9781003324690-7

TABLE 7.2

Department Table

DeptID	deptname
E1	Customer Accounting
E2	Customer Relation
E3	Customer Management
E4	Maintenance

Example: Find out the names of all those employees whose deptname is customer relation.

Query: Select empname from employee where deptID= (select deptID from department where deptname ='Customer Relation')

Output: The above query is divided into two parts: the inner query and outer query. The inner query will get the deptID whose deptname is customer relation, then the value of deptID will be compared with the outer query and display the names of employees as shown in the table 7.3.

TABLE 7.3

Selection Using Subquery 1

Empname
Shrey
Parisha

Example: Find out the names of all those employees whose deptname in customer relation or maintenance.

Query: Select empname from employee where deptID IN (select deptID from department where deptname ='Customer Relation' or deptname ='Maintenance')

Output: The above query is divided into two parts: the inner query and outer query. The inner query will get the deptID whose deptname is customer relation or maintenance, then the value of deptID will be compared with the outer query and display the names of employees. This will display the two records only as no employee in employee table has the deptID E4. Result of the above query in shown in the table 7.4.

TABLE 7.4

Selection Using Subquery 2

Empname
Shrey
Parisha

Subqueries may be used in an UPDATE statement. Since it is possible to change many values at once with a subquery.

Syntax

UPDATE table_name
SET Attribute_name = new value
WHERE attribute_name operator
(SELECT attribute_name FROM table_name WHERE [condition])

Example: Update the project names by Economics, whose deptname is customer relation.

Query: Update employee set Project= 'Economics' where deptID= (select deptID from department where deptname='Customer Relation');

Output: This will update the value of the project in the employee table 7.5 by Economics for those whose deptname is customer relation in department relation.

*Select * from employee;*

TABLE 7.5

Selection After Updating

EmpID	Empname	DeptID	City	Project
101	Amit	E1	Lucknow	Marketing
102	Shrey	E2	Dehradun	Economics
103	Parisha	E2	Delhi	Economics
104	Neha	E1	Haldwani	Marketing
105	Pranav	E3	Kanpur	Sales
106	Rohit	E3	Gorakhpur	Sales

7.2 Understanding Nested Query

A subquery can be nested inside other subqueries. SQL has the ability to nest queries within one another. A subquery is a SELECT statement nested within another SELECT statement and returns intermediate results. SQL executes the innermost subquery first, then the next level.

Syntax

Select Attribute_name(s) from table where [condition] operator ((Select Attribute_name(s) from table where [condition] operator (Select Attribute_name(s) from table where [condition]))

In the above syntax, we can see there are two subqueries, and one subquery is nested with another subquery. In this case, the innermost subquery will execute first, then the outer subquery will execute that passes the input to the outermost query.

7.3 Join Operator

The JOIN operator specifies how to relate tables in the query. With the join operator, we can get the data from multiple tables.

The following are the most common types of joins used in RDBMS shown in the figure 7.1 and 7.2:

- INNER
- OUTER (LEFT. RIGHT, FULL)
- CROSS

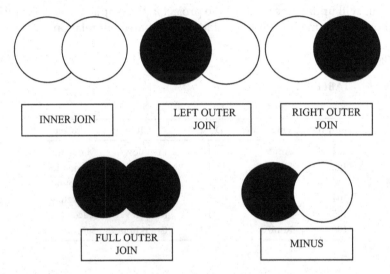

FIGURE 7.1
Types of JOIN in Database.

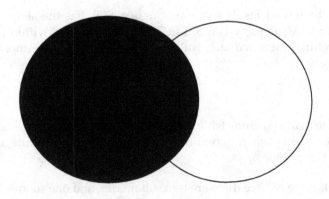

FIGURE 7.2
Left OUTER JOIN.

INNER JOIN: Select the records based on the common attribute between the two tables as per the given condition.

LEFT, RIGHT, or FULL OUTER JOIN: Select all rows from the table on the left (or right, or both) regardless of whether the other table has values in common and (usually) enter NULL where data is missing. (Note: FULL OUTER JOIN not implemented in Access.)

CROSS JOIN (not illustrated—not exactly a set operation): Select all possible combinations of rows and columns from both tables (Cartesian product). Not available in Access but can "happen" by not specifying relationships between tables or not setting up the appropriate joins in a query. (Not A Good Thing— the query may run for a very long time and produce a huge, not very useful result set.)

7.3.1 INNER JOIN

Select the records based on the common attribute between the two tables as per the given condition. It is the most widely used join operation and can be considered a default join-type. It is divided into three categories:

- Theta Join
- Equi Join
- Natural Join

Theta Join

It uses the predicate, and only those records will be displayed that satisfy the given predicate.

$$A \bowtie_\theta B$$

Let's take the following table 7.6 and table 7.7.

TABLE 7.6

A and B Tables

Table A		Table B	
Attribute1	Attribute2	Attribute1	Attribute2
1	1	1	1
1	2	1	3

$A \bowtie$ A.attribute2 > B.attribute2 (B) will generate the following result.

TABLE 7.7

Theta JOIN

Attribute1	Attribute2
1	2

EQUI JOIN

When we use an equal sign while using the predicate, it is termed as EQUI JOIN.

A ⋈ A.attribute2 = B.attribute2 (B) will generate the following results shown in the table 7.8 while applying to the above two tables A,B

TABLE 7.8

EQUI JOIN

Attribute1	Attribute2
1	1

Natural Join (⋈)

It can only be performed when joining relations will have common attributes. The attribute's name and form must be the same. Lets have two table 7.9 and table 7.10 and performing the natural join between them.

TABLE 7.9

Student1

RollNo	Student Name
1	Jagdish
2	Ravi
3	Tanupriya

TABLE 7.10

Student2

RollNo	F_Name
1	Prayag
2	Rajkumar
4	Ramesh

Student1⋈student2 will result in the following table 7.11

TABLE 7.11

Natural JOIN

RollNo	Student Name	F_Name
1	Jagdish	Prayag
2	Ravi	Rajkumar

Refer to the above employee and department table

Example: Find out the names of employee and their deptname based on the employee and department table.

Query: Select e.empname, d.deptname from employee e, department d where e.deptID= d.deptID;

Output: This will match the values of deptID between the table's employee and department and fetch the desired output shown in the table 7.12.

TABLE 7.12

Natural JOIN on Employee and Department

Empname	Deptname
Amit	Customer Accounting
Shrey	Customer Relation
Parisha	Customer Relation
Neha	Customer Accounting
Pranav	Customer Management
Rohit	Customer Management

7.3.2 SELF JOIN

A SELF JOIN is used to create a table by joining itself as if there were two tables. In SELF JOIN, we create a temporary table for executing SQL statements.

Syntax

Select Table_1.attribute_name, Table_1.Attribute_name FROM table_1 T1, Table_1.T2 WHERE T1.attribute_name < T2.attribute_name;

Here, we have created the two tables from one table and performed the SELF JOIN between them.

Refer to the above employee table.

Query: Select e.empname, e.deptID from employee e, employee e1 where e.deptID= e1.deptID;

Output: We will compare the values of deptID and display the values whose deptID is the same as we have used the equal to operator. Result of the above query is shown in table 7.13.

TABLE 7.13

SELF JOIN

Empname	DeptID
Amit	E1
Shrey	E2
Parisha	E2
Neha	E1
Pranav	E3
Rohit	E3

7.3.3 OUTER JOIN

We use the SQL OUTER JOIN to match rows between tables. OUTER JOIN is used to find the matched and unmatched records. In the previous section, we have seen how to find the matched records but unmatched records are not part of the final relation. Here we have three types of OUTER JOIN are:

- Left OUTER JOIN
- Right OUTER JOIN
- Full OUTER JOIN

7.3.3.1 Left OUTER JOIN

The left OUTER JOIN will fetch the matching records from both the relations and the unmatched records from the left-hand relation.

Syntax   Select attribute_name(s) from table1 left outer join table2 on table1.attributename = table2. Attributename;

As we can see, we will fetch the complete records from table1 and match records from table2.

Let's create the table stu1 and stu2.

```
Create table stu1
(
Roll_no integer Primary Key,
Stu_name char(10),
City char(10)
);

Create table stu2
(
Roll_no Integer Primary Key,
Sapid varchar(10)
);
```

Insert the records for stu1 table

```
Insert into stu1 values (1, 'Amit', 'Delhi');
Insert into stu1 values (2, 'Sumit', 'Mumbai')
Insert into stu1 values (3, 'Ram', 'Delhi')
Insert into stu1 values (4, 'Shayam', 'Dehradun')
Insert into stu1 values (5, 'Naina', 'Delhi')
Insert into stu1 values (6, 'Pari', 'Chennai')
```

Now retrieve the records from database for stu1 shown in table 7.14.

Select* from stu1;

TABLE 7.14

Stu1

Roll_no	Stu_name	City
1	Amit	Delhi
2	Sumit	Mumbai
3	Ram	Delhi
4	Shayam	Dehradun
5	Naina	Delhi
6	Pari	Chennai

Insert the records for stu2.

```
Insert into stu2 values (1,'S1');
Insert into stu2 values (3,'S3');
Insert into stu2 values (4,'S4');
Insert into stu2 values (6,'S6');
Insert into stu2 values (7,'S7');
Insert into stu2 values (8,'S8');
```

Now retrieve the records from the database for stu2 shown in table 7.15.

Select* from stu2;

TABLE 7.15

Stu2

Roll_no	Sapid
1	S1
3	S3
4	S4
6	S6
7	S7
8	S8

Example: Find out all the matched records from both tables.

Query: Select * from stu1, stu2 from stu1, stu2 where stu1.roll_no= stu2.roll_no;

Output: This will display all the matching records as per the table 7.16 from both tables based on the rollno.

TABLE 7.16

Natural JOIN Between stu1 and stu2

Roll_no	Stu_name	City	SapID
1	Amit	Delhi	S1
3	Ram	Delhi	S3
4	Shayam	Dehradun	S4
6	Pari	Chennai	S6

In the above result, the two records from the stu1 table are not displayed as they are not matched with table 2, so to overcome this, and if we want all the records from table 1 and matched from table 2, then we will use the outer join.

Example: Find all the matched records from both the tables, as well as unmatched records from stu1.

*Query: Select * from stu1 left outer join stu2 on stu1.roll_no= stu2.roll_no;*

Output: This will display all the matching records (shown in the table 7.17) from both the tables based on the rollno and unmatched records from stu1 because of the stu1 table is on the left side of the query. This will also fill the null values for the unmatched values of the right relation.

TABLE 7.17

Left OUTER JOIN Between stu1 and stu2

Roll_no	Stu_name	City	SapID
1	Amit	Delhi	S1
3	Ram	Delhi	S3
4	Shayam	Dehradun	S4
6	Pari	Chennai	S6
2	Sumit	Mumbai	NULL
5	Naina	Delhi	NULL

7.3.3.2 Right OUTER JOIN

The right OUTER JOIN will fetch the matching records from both the relations and the unmatched records from the right-hand relation as shown in the figure 7.3.

Syntax

Select attribute_name(s) from table1 right outer join table2 on table1.attributename = table2. Attributename;

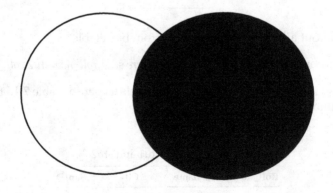

FIGURE 7.3
Right OUTER JOIN.

As we can see will fetch the complete records from table2 and matched records from table 1.

Let's consider the above table's stu1 and stu2.

Example: Find out the all the matched records from both tables.

*Select * from stu1, stu2 from stu1, stu2 where stu1.roll_no= stu2.roll_no;*

Output: This will display all the matching records (shown in the table 7.18) from both tables based on the rollno.

TABLE 7.18

Inner JOIN Between stu1 and stu2

Roll_no	Stu_name	City	SapID
1	Amit	Delhi	S1
3	Ram	Delhi	S3
4	Shayam	Dehradun	S4
6	Pari	Chennai	S6

In the above result, the two records from stu2 table are not displayed as they are not matched with Table 7.14, so to overcome this, if we want all the records from table 2 and matched from Table 7.15, then we will use the right outer join.

Example: Find out all the matched records from both the tables, as well as unmatched records from stu2.

*Query:Select * from stu1 right outer join stu2 on stu1.roll_no= stu2.roll_no;*

Output: This will display all the matching records (shown in the table 7.19) from both the tables based on the rollno and unmatched records from stu2 because of the stu2 table is on the right side of the query. This will also fill the null values for the unmatched values of the left relation.

TABLE 7.19

Right OUTER JOIN Between stu1 and stu2

Roll_no	Stu_name	City	SapID
1	Amit	Delhi	S1
3	Ram	Delhi	S3
4	Shayam	Dehradun	S4
6	Pari	Chennai	S6
7	NULL	NULL	S7
8	NULL	NULL	S8

7.3.3.3 *Full OUTER JOIN*

The full OUTER JOIN will fetch the matching, as well as unmatched records for both the relations.

Syntax

Select attribute_name(s) from table1 full outer join table2 on table1.attributename = table2. Attributename;

Let's consider the above two tables stu1 and stu2

Example: Find out all the matched and unmatched records from both the tables.

*Query: Select * from stu1 full outer join stu2 on stu1.roll_no= stu2.roll_no;*

Output: This will display all the matching as well as unmatched records (shown in the table 7.20) from both the tables based on the rollno. In this form of outer join, we will get all the records, so no records are left to display from both the tables.

TABLE 7.20

Full OUTER JOIN Between stu1 and stu2

Roll_no	Stu_name	City	SapID
1	Amit	Delhi	S1
3	Ram	Delhi	S3
4	Shayam	Dehradun	S4
6	Pari	Chennai	S6
7	NULL	NULL	S7
8	NULL	NULL	S8
2	Sumit	Mumbai	NULL
5	Naina	Delhi	NULL

7.4 Summary

Use both JOINS and subqueries to fetch the data from different tables. Though they may even share the same query plan, they have a different approach for fetching the records from multiple tables, as shown in the chapter. A subquery has two different parts: the first part is known as inner query and the second part is known as outer query. The inner query will be inside the outer query and executed first. If one subquery is within another subquery, it is known as a nested subquery. The various types of JOINS are also used to fetch the records from multiple tables, known as INNER JOIN and OUTER JOIN. The OUTER JOIN is further divided into two types: left OUTER JOIN and right OUTER JOIN.

References

1. Oracle Web Page, 'PL/SQL LOB Types', [Online]. Available: https://docs.oracle.com/cd/B19306_01/appdev.102/b14261/datatypes.htm#i43142. [Accessed: 07 Febuary 2022].
2. 'Performing SQL Operations from PL/SQL', [Online]. Available: https://docs.oracle.com/cd/B19306_01/appdev.102/b14261/sqloperations.htm#i7106. [Accessed: 17 April 2022].

3. Oracle Web Page, 'PL/SQL Types', [Online]. Available: https://docs.oracle.com/cd/B19306_01/appdev.102/b14261/datatypes.htm#i46029.
4. Patni, J.C., Sharma, H.K., Tomar, R., & Katal, A. (2022). *Database Management System: An Evolutionary Approach* (1st ed.). Chapman and Hall/CRC. https://doi.org/10.1201/9780429282843
5. 'Subqueries and Joins', [Online]. Available: https://www.ibm.com/docs/en/db2/10.5?topic=table-examples-subselect-queries-joins, [Accessed: 07 January 2022].
6. 'Nested Join', [Online]. Available: https://dev.mysql.com/doc/refman/8.0/en/nested-join-optimization.html, [Accessed: 17 January 2022].
7. 'SQL Subquery', [Online]. Available: https://www.sqltutorial.org/sql-subquery/, [Accessed: 23 January 2022].
8. 'Subqueries Vs. Join', [Online]. Available: https://www.essentialsql.com/what-is-the-difference-between-a-join-and-subquery/, [Accessed: 28 January 2022].

8

Views, Indexes, and Sequence

Views, indexes, and sequences are the advanced concepts of database systems and are used to maintain additional security, more flexible uses, lesser complexity, and most importantly, faster storage and retrieval of records from the database.

8.1 Introduction to VIEW

A VIEW is not a physical table, rather, it is in essence a virtual table created by a query joining one or more tables. A view can be created as per the requirement and conditions given in the query.

Views do not have any data stored in the database; it is only the image of a table or multiple tables. We can perform the data manipulation operations from views. A view will be created over the table and have a name. A view will fetch the records from the database using similar queries we used with tables. We can allow users to get the data from the VIEW, and the user does not require permission for each table or column to fetch data.

In the following image, you can see the VIEW contains a query to join three relational tables and fetch the data in a virtual table.

The views as shown in the figure 8.1 have the following advantages

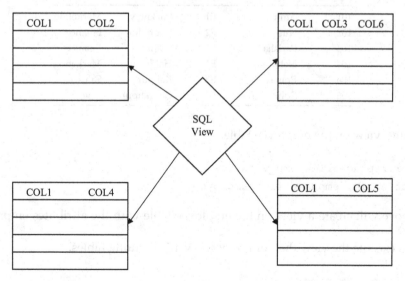

FIGURE 8.1
View structure.

DOI: 10.1201/9781003324690-8

8.2 Types of Views

A view will be divided into two categories based on the design structure known as:

- Simple View
- Composite View

8.2.1 Simple View

A view with a single base table is called a simple view, or we can say that if only one table is associated in the view is called a simple view.

Create View

Syntax

```
Create or replace view view_name
As select attributes_name(s) from table_name
Where [condition];
```

The replace will work if an already existing view is there. This will replace the existing view with the new definitions, otherwise, using create it will return an error as view already exists.

Refer to the following employee table 8.1.

TABLE 8.1

Employee Table

EmpID	Empname	DeptID	City	Project
101	Amit	E1	Lucknow	Marketing
102	Shrey	E2	Dehradun	Finance
103	Parisha	E2	Delhi	Finance
104	Neha	E1	Haldwani	Marketing
105	Pranav	E3	Kanpur	Sales
106	Rohit	E3	Gorakhpur	Sales

Let's create a view on the employee table.

```
Create or replace view emp_view
As select empID, empname from employee;
```

The above will create a view on the employee table with the attributes empname and empID.

We will execute the view the same way we were executing tables.

```
Select* from view_name;

Select* from emp_view
```

Output: shown in the table 8.2.

View: emp_view

TABLE 8.2

emp_view

EmpID	Empname
101	Amit
102	Shrey
103	Parisha
104	Neha
105	Pranav
106	Rohit

Example: Create and display the view_emp having the empname and deptID for those employees whose empID is greater than 102.

Query:

Create or replace view view_emp

As select empname, deptID from employee where empID >102;

Output: shown in the table 8.3.

Select* from view_emp;

TABLE 8.3

View_emp

Empname	DeptID
Parisha	E2
Neha	E1
Pranav	E3
Rohit	E3

Update VIEW

We can modify the definition of a VIEW in SQL without dropping it by using the ALTER VIEW statement. As we have used ALTER statement to modify the schema, in the same way, we can modify the view.

Syntax

```
Alter view view_name As Select attribute_name(s) from table_name where
[condition]
Alter view view_emp
As select empname, deptID, city from employee where empID >102;
```

Output: Here, we have added one more attribute in the view, so now the view is modified and has three attributes instead of two. Results are shown in table 8.4.

Select * from view_emp;

TABLE 8.4

Updated View

Empname	DeptID	City
Parisha	E2	Delhi
Neha	E1	Haldwani
Pranav	E3	Kanpur
Rohit	E3	Gorakhpur

Drop View

After creating the view, if we do not need the view, then we can drop the view by the drop command.

Syntax

Drop view view_name;

Insert via View

We can insert the records via view, but we have to ensure that all the attributes that are not part of the view must be null in the table definition. If the attributes are not null in the table definition, then they must need the values, but from view, we can only enter the values for those attributes defined in the view. In such cases, the errors will reflect, and records will not be inserted. The records inserted via view will be stored in the base relation only, not in the view, as view can't store any records due to the virtual table only.

Syntax

Insert into view_name values(Attribute1_value, ...attributeN-Value);

Example: insert the three values in the employee table via the emp-View.

```
Insert into emp_view values (107,'Jagdish');
Insert into emp_view values (108,'Pooja');
Insert into emp_view values (109,'Rakesh');
```

Now we have inserted the three records via emp_view by assuming the rest of the employee attributes have the null property.

Now fetching the records from the employee table will have the following query and output.

Select* from employee;

Output: shown in the table 8.5.

TABLE 8.5

Employee Table After Adding Records from View

EmpID	Empname	DeptID	City	Project
101	Amit	E1	Lucknow	Marketing
102	Shrey	E2	Dehradun	Finance
103	Parisha	E2	Delhi	Finance

(Continued)

TABLE 8.5 (CONTINUED)

Employee Table After Adding Records from View

EmpID	Empname	DeptID	City	Project
104	Neha	E1	Haldwani	Marketing
105	Pranav	E3	Kanpur	Sales
106	Rohit	E3	Gorakhpur	Sales
107	Jagdish	NULL	NULL	NULL
108	Pooja	NULL	NULL	NULL
109	Rakesh	NULL	NULL	NULL

8.2.2 Composite View

If a view has multiple base relations, then it is called a composite view. Here, view will be created by joining two or more relations based on the common attribute.

Create View

Syntax

```
Create or replace view view_name
As select attributes_name(s) from table_name1, table_name2
Where [condition];
```

The replace will work if an already existing view is there. This will replace the existing view with the new definitions; otherwise, using create it will return error as view already exists.

Refer to the above employee table.

Let's create a view on the employee table.

```
Create or replace view emp_view
As select empID, empname, deptname from employee, department
Where employee.deptID=department.deptID;
```

The above will create a view on the employee table with the attributes empname empID and deptname.

We will execute the view the same way we were executing tables.

```
Select* from view_name;
```

```
Select* from emp_view
```

Output: shown in the table 8.6.

View: emp_view

TABLE 8.6

Composite View

EmpID	Empname	deptname
101	Amit	Customer Accounting
102	Shrey	Customer Relation
103	Parisha	Customer Relation
104	Neha	Customer Accounting
105	Pranav	Customer Management
106	Rohit	Customer Management

Example: Create and display the view_emp having the empname, empID, and deptname for those employees whose empID is greater than 102.

Query:

Create or replace view view_emp

As select empname, empID,deptname from employee, department where employee.deptID=
*   department.deptID and employee.empID >102;*

Output: shown in the table 8.7.

Select* from view_emp;

TABLE 8.7

Composite View Using Where Clause

EmpID	Empname	deptname
103	Parisha	Customer Relation
104	Neha	Customer Accounting
105	Pranav	Customer Management
106	Rohit	Customer Management

Update VIEW

We can modify the definition of a VIEW in SQL without dropping it by using the ALTER VIEW statement. As we have used ALTER statement to modify the schema, in the same way we can modify the view.

Syntax

Alter view view_name As Select attribute_name(s) from table1_name, table2_name
    where [condition]

Drop View

After creating the view, if we do not need the view, then we can drop the view by the drop command.

Syntax

Drop view view_name;

Insert via View

We can insert the records via view, but we have to ensure that all the attributes that are not part of view must be null in table definition. If the attributes are not null in the table definition, then they must need the values; but from view, we can only enter the values for those attributes defined in the view. In such cases, the errors will reflect, and records will not be inserted. The records inserted via view will be stored in the base relation only, not in the view, as the view can't store any records due to the virtual table only.

Syntax

Insert into view_name values(Attribute1_value, ...attributeN-Value);
Example: Insert the three values in the employee table via the emp-view.

```
Insert into emp_view values (107, 'Jagdish');
Insert into emp_view values (108, 'Pooja');
Insert into emp_view values (109, 'Rakesh');
```

Now we have inserted the three records via emp_view by assuming the rest of the employee attributes have the null property.

Now fetching the records from the employee table will have the following query and output.

Select* from employee;

Output: shown in the table 8.8.

TABLE 8.8

Insert via View

EmpID	Empname	DeptID	City	Project
101	Amit	E1	Lucknow	Marketing
102	Shrey	E2	Dehradun	Finance
103	Parisha	E2	Delhi	Finance
104	Neha	E1	Haldwani	Marketing
105	Pranav	E3	Kanpur	Sales
106	Rohit	E3	Gorakhpur	Sales
107	Jagdish	NULL	NULL	NULL
108	Pooja	NULL	NULL	NULL
109	Rakesh	NULL	NULL	NULL

8.3 Indexes

A database index is a data structure that improves the speed of operations in a table. Indexes can be created using one or more columns, providing the basis for faster lookups and efficiently ordering access to records.

While creating index, it should be taken into consideration which all columns will be used to make SQL queries and create one or more indexes on those columns.

Indexes are also tables known as lookup table where the indexed attribute and its address is stored.

As the user can't see the index table, results will be faster by using indexes.

The INSERT and UPDATE statements take more time on tables having indexes, whereas the SELECT statements become fast on those tables. The reason is that while doing insert or update, a database needs to insert or update the index values as well.

8.4 Types of Index

Indexes are divided on various types based on its functionality and storage mechanism. The following indexes used here are:

- Simple Index
- Composite Index
- Unique Index
- Reverse Index
- Function-based Index

8.4.1 Simple Index

Index will be created to retrieve the records faster, and if we are creating the index on a single attribute, it is called simple index.

Syntax

Create index index_name on Table_name (attribute_name)

Refer to the above employee table

Create index emp_index on employee (empname);

Output:

Index created

This will create an index on the attribute empname. It means that when we want to retrieve the records based on the value of empname, it will search the index value on the index table and retrieve the records faster.

8.4.2 Composite Index

If we are creating the index on multiple attributes from a single relation, it is called composite index.

Syntax

Create index index_name on Table_name (attribute1_name, attribute2_name.......... attributeN_name)

Refer to the above employee table.

Create index emp_index on employee (empname, city);

Output:

Index created

This will create an index on the attribute empname and city. It means that when we want to retrieve the records based on the value of empname and city, it will search the index value on the index table and retrieve the records faster.

Note: Primary key attribute(s) are automatically indexed, so we need not create the index on such attributes. If an index is already created on attribute(s), no further index will be created on the same, and if we need to create a new index with new definitions, then we have to drop the previous index.

8.4.3 Unique Index

Unique index is the same as a simple or composite index, but only one difference is if an index is created for a search key, then no further index will be created for the same value of the attribute. For example, if we have created a unique index on empname, then all the values of empname will be unique as no index will be created for the duplicate values of empname.

Syntax

Create unique index index_name on Table_name (attribute_name)
   Or

Create unique index index_name on Table_name (attribute1_name, attribute2_ name..........attributeN_name)

Refer to the above employee table

Create unique index emp_index on employee (empname);

Output:
Index Created

This will create a unique index on the attribute empname. It means that only unique values of empnames will be indexed; if more than one value with the same name, then the record will be rejected.

8.4.4 Reverse Index

Reverse index is used to reverse the value of the index, which will help for faster retrieval of records as once the indexed is reversed, all the values will be changed because all the records are stored in different blocks. As the records are stored on different blocks, it will help us to retrieve multiple records at the same time.

Syntax

Create index index_name on Table_name (attribute_name) reverse;
   Or

Create index index_name on Table_name (attribute1_name, attribute2_name..........
   attributeN_name) reverse;

Refer to the above employee table.

Create reverse index emp_index on employee (empname);

Output:

Index Created

This will create an indexe on the attribute empname, and while storing the records, it will reverse the values of index.

For example, the above index table 8.9 will have the following values.

TABLE 8.9

Index on Employee

Empname	Index value
Amit	11
Shrey	12
Parisha	13
Neha	14
Pranav	15
Rohit	16

The reverse index will reverse the value of index and the new values of address will be as per the following table 8.10.

TABLE 8.10

Reverse Index

Empname	Index Value
Amit	11
Shrey	21
Parisha	31
Neha	41
Pranav	51
Rohit	61

If we refer to the first number as the block number, then all the records are stored in the different blocks as compared to the regular index will store all the records in the same block.

8.4.5 Function-Based Index

Function-based index is used to store the records in specific conditions like upper case of the values of empname.

Refer to the above employee table.

Create index emp_index on employee (UPPER(empname));

Output:

Index created

This will store all the values of empname in the upper case letters in the index table.

Create index emp_index on employee (LOWER(empname));

This will store all the value of empname in the lower case letters in the index table.

Note: We can alter and drop the indexes by the similar methods that we were using for tables or views.

8.5 Sequences

A sequence is a series of numbers defined in some specific order like 1,2,3...100 or 2,4,6...100. Sequences are used to provide the numbers between the multiple tables uniquely. A sequence can be used by multiple tables.

The syntax of the sequence

```
Create sequence sequence_name
Start with value
Increment by value
Max value value;
```

8.6 Types of Sequences

Sequences are categorized mainly in three types are:

1. Auto-Increment
2. Cycle
3. No cycle

8.6.1 Auto-Increment Sequence

The auto-increment sequences are used to automatically provide the sequences by the database. Here, we need not declare any conditions.

Syntax

```
Create Table Table_name
(
Attribute_name type  Primary Key Auto Increment,
Attribute_name type
);
```

Let's take an example of auto-increment sequence for the following student relation.

```
Create table student
(
Srno integer auto increment,
```

```
Roll_no integer Primary Key,
Name char(10) not null,
Sapid varchar(10)
);
```

In the above table, we have defined the auto-increment sequence for srno attribute, so we need not give the value during insert into command.

Let's insert the records with auto-increment sequence

```
Insert into student values(NULL,11,'Amit', 'S1');
Insert into student values(NULL,12,'Ram', 'S2');
Insert into student values(NULL,13,'Sunil', 'S3');
Insert into student values(NULL,14,'Madhav, 'S4');
Insert into student values(NULL,15,'Rohit', 'S5');
Insert into student values(NULL,16,'Jatin', 'S6');
```

In the above insert into command, we have not given the values for srno, but the values will automatically retrieve from the auto-increment sequence.

Select* from student;

Output: shown in the table 8.11.

TABLE 8.11

Student Table

Srno	Rollno	Name	sapid
1	11	Amit	S1
2	12	Ram	S2
3	13	Sunil	S3
4	14	Madhav	S4
5	15	Rohit	S5
6	16	Jatin	S6

8.6.2 Cycle Sequence

This type of sequence is used to reuse the values of sequences once we reach the maximum value, or the sequences is exhausted.

Syntax

```
Create sequence sequence_name
Start with value
Increment by value
Max value value
Cycle;
```

Let's take an example.

```
Create sequence sequence_stu
Start with 1
Increment by 1
Max value 100
Cycle;
```

Output:

Sequence Created

The above sequence will have the start value of 1, and every time the value is increased by 1 with the maximum value of 100. Once it reaches the maximum value 100, the sequence will stop assigning the sequences, but the cycle function will again start with 1 once all the sequences are exhausted.

8.6.3 No Cycle Sequence

This type of sequence will stop assigning the sequences once it reaches the maximum value.

Syntax

```
Create sequence sequence_name
Start with value
Increment by value
Max value value
No Cycle;
```

Let's take an example.

```
Create sequence sequence_stu
Start with 1
Increment by 1
Max value 100
No Cycle;
```

Output:

Sequence Created

The above sequence will have the start value of 1, and every time the value is increased by 1 with the maximum value of 100. Once it reaches the maximum value 100, the sequence will stop assigning the sequences.

8.7 Examples

Further we can use the sequences to add the values from the sequences to the base table. For this purpose, we are using two functions of sequences.

- Nextval: This will retrieve the next value of the sequence.

Syntax

Select Sequence_name.nextval from dummy table;

- Currval: This will retrieve the current value of the sequence.

Select Sequence_name.currval from dummy table;
Let's create a student table and enter the values from sequences.

```
Create table student
(
Srno integer auto increment,
Roll_no integer Primary Key,
Name char(10) not null,
Sapid varchar(10)
);
```

Table created

Let's create a sequence

```
Create sequence sequence_stu
Start with 1
Increment by 1
Max value 100
No Cycle;
```

Sequence Created

Now in the above employee table, we will store the values from sequences.

```
Insert into student values(Sequence_stu.nextval,11,'Amit', 'S1');
Insert into student values(Sequence_stu.nextval,12,'Ram', 'S2');
Insert into student values(Sequence_stu.nextval,13,'Sunil', 'S3');
Insert into student values(Sequence_stu.nextval,14,'Madhav', 'S4');
Insert into student values(Sequence_stu.nextval,15,'Rohit', 'S5');
Insert into student values(Sequence_stu.nextval,16,'Jatin', 'S6');
```

Let's the sequence be empty initially and start assigning the values starting with 1.

Select* from student; results as per the table 8.12.

TABLE 8.12

Student Table Created via Sequences

Srno	Rollno	Name	sapid
1	11	Amit	S1
2	12	Ram	S2
3	13	Sunil	S3
4	14	Madhav	S4
5	15	Rohit	S5
6	16	Jatin	S6

8.8 Summary

This chapter describes the advanced concepts of database systems, including views, indexes, and sequences. We have implemented different types of indexes, views, and sequences with proper syntax and examples. Views are used as an image of a table, and we can use them for a specific purpose to secure the system and make it easy to use. Indexes are used to easily store and efficiently retrieve records from database. We have discussed different types of indexes that are used for efficient and effective retrieval of records. Sequences are a series of numbers used among multiple tables. Cycle is used to repeat the sequences and no cycle, that is stopped once sequences are exhausted.

References

1. Oracle Web Page, 'PL/SQL LOB Types', [Online]. Available: https://docs.oracle.com/cd/B19306_01/appdev.102/b14261/datatypes.htm#i43142, [Accessed: 07 January 2022].
2. 'Performing SQL Operations from PL/SQL', [Online]. Available: https://docs.oracle.com/cd/B19306_01/appdev.102/b14261/sqloperations.htm#i7106, [Accessed: 22 January 2021].
3. Oracle Web Page, 'PL/SQL Types', [Online]. Available: https://docs.oracle.com/cd/B19306_01/appdev.102/b14261/datatypes.htm#i46029.
4. Patni, J.C., Sharma, H.K., Tomar, R., & Katal, A. (2022). *Database Management System: An Evolutionary Approach* (1st ed.). Chapman and Hall/CRC. https://doi.org/10.1201/9780429282843
5. 'SQL Server Create View', [online]. Available: https://www.sqlservertutorial.net/sql-server-views/sql-server-create-view/, [Accessed: 23 March 2022].
6. 'Views in SQL', [online]. Available: https://www.javatpoint.com/dbms-sql-view, [Accessed: 11 January 2022].
7. 'Create View', [online]. Available: https://docs.microsoft.com/en-us/sql/t-sql/statements/create-view-transact-sql?view=sql-server-ver15, [Accessed: 13 January 2022].
8. 'SQL Indexes', [online]. Available: https://www.javatpoint.com/dbms-sql-index, [Accessed: 11 January 2022].
9. 'SQL Server Indexes', [online]. Available: https://www.sqlservertutorial.net/sql-server-indexes/, [Accessed: 23 March 2022].
10. Create Sequence, 'Database SQL Reference', [online]. Available: https://docs.oracle.com/cd/B19306_01/server.102/b14200/statements_6015.htm, [Accessed: 23 April 2022].

9

PL/SQL

9.1 Introduction to PL/SQL

PL/SQL is a block-structured language that can have multiple blocks in it. In this chapter, we discuss the basics of PL/SQL with data types, constant, variables, and examples related to PL/SQL.

1. PL/SQL is a completely portable, high-performance transaction-processing language.
2. PL/SQL provides a built-in, interpreted, and OS-independent programming environment.
3. PL/SQL can also directly be called from the command-line SQL interface.
4. Direct calls can also be made from external programming language calls to the database.

9.2 Features of PL/SQL

The PL/SQL includes the functionalities provided by most programming languages, such as declaring variables, constants, conditional statements, loops, and supports triggers. Advanced techniques like exception handling and array data structure are also supported. In a later version of Oracle, even object-oriented features are made available to PL/SQL. The important thing to know and remember about PL/SQL is that these programs are stored and executed on DBMS only. They can be triggered based upon changes in value on tables. This helps in processing the data in near real-time on the database itself.

Unlike other procedural languages, PL/SQL is not case sensitive, and you can use any combination of lower case and upper case letters. The lexical units composed of characters in a line of PL/SQL text can be classified into delimiters, identifiers, literals, and comments.

PL/SQL is programming logic in SQL has similar logic that we have used with other programming languages. The following are the features of PL/SQL.

- PL/SQL is integrated with SQL and uses the concepts of SQL.
- It offers error handling and error checking.
- It has various types of data types as SQL has.

DOI: 10.1201/9781003324690-9

- Various programming interfaces and concepts.
- It supports the programming concepts like function, procedures, cursors, triggers, etc.
- It also supports the object-oriented programming.
- It is used for server site programming to develop web applications.

9.3 Advantages of PL/SQL

PL/SQL has the following advantages:

1. SQL is the standard database language, and PL/SQL is strongly integrated with SQL. PL/SQL supports both static and dynamic SQL. Static SQL supports DML operations and transaction control from PL/SQL block. In dynamic SQL, SQL allows embedding DDL statements in PL/SQL blocks.

2. PL/SQL allows sending an entire block of statements to the database simultaneously. This reduces network traffic and provides high performance for the applications.

3. PL/SQL gives high productivity to programmers as it can query, transform, and update data in a database.

4. PL/SQL saves time on design and debugging through strong features, such as exception handling, encapsulation, data hiding, and object-oriented data types.

5. Applications written in PL/SQL are fully portable.

6. PL/SQL provides a high-security level.

7. PL/SQL provides access to predefined SQL packages.

8. PL/SQL provides support for Object-Oriented Programming.

9. PL/SQL supports developing Web Applications and Server Pages.

9.4 Data Types in PL/SQL

Predefined PL/SQL data types are grouped into composite, LOB, reference, and scalar type categories.

- A composite type has internal components that can be manipulated individually, such as the elements of an array, record, or table.
- A LOB type holds values called lob locators that specify the location of large objects, such as text blocks or graphic images, that are stored separately from other database data. LOB types include BFILE, BLOB, CLOB, and NCLOB.
- A reference type holds values called pointers that designate other program items. These types include REF CURSORS and REFs to object types.

- A scalar type has no internal components. It holds a single value, such as a number or character string. The scalar types fall into four families, which store number, character, Boolean, and date/time data. The scalar families with their data types are:

PL/SQL Number Types

BINARY_DOUBLE, BINARY_FLOAT, BINARY_INTEGER, DEC, DECIMAL, DOUBLE PRECISION, FLOAT, INT, INTEGER, NATURAL, NATURALN, NUMBER, NUMERIC, PLS_INTEGER, POSITIVE, POSITIVEN, REAL, SIGNTYPE, SMALLINT

PL/SQL Character and String Types and PL/SQL National Character Types CHAR, CHARACTER, LONG, LONG RAW, NCHAR, NVARCHAR2, RAW, ROWID, STRING, UROWID, VARCHAR, VARCHAR2

"LONG and LONG RAW Datatypes" The LONG and LONG RAW data types are supported only for backward compatibility;

PL/SQL Date, Time, and Interval Types DATE, TIMESTAMP, TIMESTAMP WITH TIMEZONE, TIMESTAMP WITH LOCAL TIMEZONE, INTERVAL YEAR TO MONTH, INTERVAL DAY TOSECOND

NULLs in PL/SQL PL/SQL NULL values represent **missing** or **unknown data** and are not an integer, a character, or any other specific data type. Note that **NULL** is not the same as an empty data string or the null character value "\0". A null can be assigned, but cannot be equated with anything, including itself.

9.5 Variables and Constants

Similar to other programming languages, PL/SQL also uses variables to store the temporary state of the program. In other words, we can say that variable is a meaningful name given to the storage memory. Variables are used to manipulate the data during the execution of the program. The variables have a data type and size that define what kind of data and how much data can be stored inside one variable. Few points to remember about variables:

- The naming rule states that the name of a variable should not exceed 30 characters.
- The first letter should be any letter only, followed by any alphanumeric, dollar sign, and underscore.
- The dollar sign and underscore are provided to create readability in the long variable name.
- The variable names are not case-sensitive.
- The variable should be declared in the declaration section of PL/SQL block.
- A reserved PL/SQL keyword cannot be used as a variable name.
- NOT NULL is an optional specification on the variable.

The variable is defined in the declaration section of the program. The variable, by default, comprises a NULL value, and to initialize it with some initial value, we can either use the assignment operator (:=) or the DEFAULT keyword. The syntax with example is shown below.

```
variableName DataType := initial_Value
for e.g. salary intger:=20000
or
variableName DataType DEFAULT initial_Value
for e.g. salary integer DEFAULT 20000
```

The PL/SQL allows the nesting of blocks. A program block can contain another inner block. If you declare a variable within an inner block, it is not accessible to an outer block. There are two types of variable scope:

- Local Variable: Local variables are the inner block variables that are not accessible to outer blocks.
- Global Variable: Global variables are declared in the outermost block.

Constant

The constants are special identifiers whose values do not change once specified. The special keyword CONSTANT is written after the identifier's name to make it constant. For example:

   PI CONSTANT real: =3.14

9.6 PL/SQL Literals

Literals are the explicit numeric, character, string, or Boolean values not represented by an identifier. For example: TRUE, NULL, etc., are all literals of type Boolean. PL/SQL literals are case-sensitive. There are the following literals as shown in Table 9.1 in PL/SQL:

- Numeric Literals
- Character Literals
- String Literals
- Boolean Literals
- Date and Time Literals

TABLE 9.1

Example of Different Types of Literals

Literals	Examples
Numeric	75125, 3568, 33.3333333 etc.
Character	'A' '%' '9' ' ' 'z' '('
String	Hello JavaTpoint!
Boolean	TRUE, FALSE, NULL, etc.
Date and Time	'26-11-2002', '2012-10-29 12:01:01'

9.7 Examples

Most of the time, in any procedural program, we encounter situation where some decision needs to be taken before executing the next statement, and/or the need for repetition of code is there. Almost every programming language supports conditional statements and loop statements. Similarly, PL/SQL supports programming language features like conditional statements and iterative statements. The syntax is very similar to any other procedural language.

9.7.1 IF Statement

If is used for conditional statements, where we can define multiple blocks in the code that executes based upon conditions. If statements can be classified into different types based on requirements. All if statements take a Boolean condition, and based upon its evaluation, the required block gets executed.

9.7.1.1 IF-THEN Statement

This will execute the statement once the condition goes true.

```
1. IF condition
2. THEN
3. Statement: {It is executed when condition is true}
4. END IF;
```

9.7.1.2 IF-THEN-ELSE Statement

This will execute the statement once the condition goes true, and if the condition goes wrong, then the control passes to the else statement.

```
1. IF condition
2. THEN
3.   {...statements to execute when condition is TRUE...}
4. ELSE
5.   {...statements to execute when condition is FALSE...}
6. END IF;
```

Syntax: (IF-THEN-ELSIF statement): This is also called the nested if where we have multiple if statement based on multiple conditions.

```
1. IF condition1
2. THEN
3.   {...statements to execute when condition1 is TRUE...}
4. ELSIF condition2
5. THEN
6.   {...statements to execute when condition2 is TRUE...}
7. END IF;
```

Syntax: (IF-THEN-ELSIF-ELSE statement): This is used when multiple statement or block needs to be executed based on multiple conditions, and there is one last condition that executes if all previously provided conditions are false.

```
1. IF condition1
2. THEN
3.   {...statements to execute when condition1 is TRUE...}
4. ELSIF condition2
5. THEN
6.   {...statements to execute when condition2 is TRUE...}
7. ELSE
8.   {...statements to execute when both condition1 and condition2 are
FALSE...}
9. END IF;
```

Example of PL/SQL If Statement

Let's take an example to see the whole concept:

```
1. DECLARE
2.    age number(2) := 20;
3. BEGIN
4.    --check for ram age to be eligible for voting
5.    IF( age < 18 ) THEN
6.       -if  age is less than 18
7.       dbms_output.put_line('Not eligible ' );
8.    ELSE
9.       dbms_output.put_line('Eligible ' );
10.    END IF;
11.    dbms_output.put_line('The age is : ' || age);
12. END;
```

After the execution of the above code in SQL prompt, you will get the following result:

Eligible to Vote
The age is : 20

PL/SQL procedure successfully completed.

9.7.2 Case Statement

The case statements are similar to switch cases in procedural languages. The case statement in PL/SQL is used when there are many else if conditions and the comparison needs to make is "equality."

The "CASE" statement takes the expression and evaluates it against provided "WHEN" conditions. Whenever a case expression is matched with WHEN, it executes the corresponding THEN part and ignores the other. If there is no WHEN part is matched, in that case the ELSE part is executed.

Syntax for the CASE Statement

```
1. CASE [ expression ]
2. WHEN condition_1 THEN result_1
3.   WHEN condition_2 THEN result_2
4.   ...
5.   WHEN condition_n THEN result_n
6. ELSE result
7. END
```

Example of PL/SQL Case Statement

Let's take an example to make it clear:

```
1.  DECLARE
2.    day number(1) := 2;
3.  BEGIN
4.    CASE day
5.      when 1 then dbms_output.put_line(Sunday);
6.      when 2 then dbms_output.put_line(Monday);
7.      when 3 then dbms_output.put_line(Tuesday);
8.      when 4 then dbms_output.put_line(Wednesday);
9.      when 5 then dbms_output.put_line('Thursday');
10.     when 6 then dbms_output.put_line('Friday');
11.     when 7 then dbms_output.put_line('Saturday');
12.     else dbms_output.put_line(Invalid Day);
13.   END CASE;
14. END;
```

After the execution of the above code, you will get the following result:

Monday
PL/SQL procedure successfully completed.

9.7.3 Loop Statement

The PL/SQL loops are used when a block of statement is required to be repeated several times. Generally, the loop will have a control variable that contains the initial value, a termination condition, and an expression that changes the control variable.

Without specifying the termination condition, we may lead the loop to an infinite condition. PL/SQL features four types of loops.

1. Basic Loop/Exit Loop
2. While Loop
3. For Loop
4. Cursor For Loop

Syntax (Basic Loop/Exit Loop)

This loop consists of an exit condition that terminates the loop. If the termination condition is not specified, then the loop becomes infinite loop.

```
1. LOOP
2.    statements;
3.    EXIT;
4.    {or EXIT WHEN condition;}
5. END LOOP;
```

The following points needs to be considered while creating the loop:

- Initialize a variable before the loop body
- Increment the variable in the loop.
- You should use EXIT with the WHEN or IF statement as demonstrated in the examples below.

Example of PL/SQL EXIT Loop with WHEN condition

Let's take a simple example to explain it well:

```
1. DECLARE
2. i NUMBER := 2;
3. BEGIN
4. LOOP
5. EXIT WHEN i>20;
6. DBMS_OUTPUT.PUT_LINE(i);
7. i := i+2;
8. END LOOP;
9. END;
```

After the execution of the above code, you will get the following result:
Output:

```
2
4
6
8
10
12
14
16
18
20
```

PL/SQL EXIT Loop Example with IF condition

```
1.  DECLARE
2.  x NUMBER;
3.  y NUMBER;
4.  BEGIN
5.  x:=10;
6.  y:=1;
7.  LOOP
8.  DBMS_OUTPUT.PUT_LINE (x*y);
9.  IF (y=10) THEN
10. EXIT;
11. END IF;
12. y:=y+1;
13. END LOOP;
14. END;
```

Output:

```
10
20
30
40
50
60
70
80
90
100
```

Syntax (While Loop)

This type of loop starts with a condition, and the condition is checked before the execution of the first statement. The statements repeat themselves until the condition is true.

Syntax of While Loop:

```
1.  WHILE <condition>
2.  LOOP statements;
3.  END LOOP;
```

The following points needs to be considered while creating the while loop:

- Initialize a variable before the loop body.
- Increment the variable in the loop.
- The use of EXIT with the WHEN or IF statement is optional in the while loop.

Example of PL/SQL While Loop

Let's see a simple example of PL/SQL WHILE loop.

```
1. DECLARE
2. i INTEGER := 2;
3. BEGIN
4. WHILE i <= 20 LOOP
5. DBMS_OUTPUT.PUT_LINE(i);
6. i := i+2;
7. END LOOP;
8. END;
```

After the execution of the above code, you will get the following result:

Output:

```
2
4
6
8
10
12
14
16
18
20
```

PL/SQL While Loop Example 2

```
1. DECLARE
2. x NUMBER;
3. y NUMBER;
4. BEGIN
5. x:=10;
6. y:=1;
7. WHILE (y<=10)
8. LOOP
9. DBMS_OUTPUT.PUT_LINE (x*y);
10. y:=y+1;
11. END LOOP;
12. END;
```

Output:

```
10
20
```

```
30
40
50
60
70
80
90
100
```

Syntax (FOR Loop)

This type of loop is most preferred because of simplicity. The loop automatically iterates between the initial and final values. The only point to remember is that this is used only for incrementing value by 1.

```
1. FOR counter IN initial_value .. final_value LOOP
2.   LOOP statements;
3. END LOOP;
```

Where,

initial_value : Start integer value

final_value : End integer value

Following points needs to be considered while creating the while loop:

- Counter variable is not required to be created; it is automatically created.
- The counter variable is always incremented by 1.
- Usage of EXIT with the WHEN or IF statement is optional in the while loop.

PL/SQL For Loop Example 1

Let's see a simple example of PL/SQL FOR loop.

```
1. BEGIN
2. FOR i IN 1..5 LOOP
3. DBMS_OUTPUT.PUT_LINE(i);
4. END LOOP;
5. END;
```

Output:

```
1
2
3
4
5
```

PL/SQL For Loop REVERSE Example

Let's see an example of PL/SQL for loop where we are using REVERSE keyword.

```
1. DECLARE
2. x NUMBER;
3. BEGIN
4. x:=10;
5. FOR i IN REVERSE 1..10
6. LOOP
7. DBMS_OUTPUT.PUT_LINE (x*i);
8. END LOOP;
9. END;
```

Output:

```
100
90
80
70
60
50
40
30
20
10
```

9.7.4 Continue Statement

The continue statement is similar to the continue statement in procedural languages. The control skips all the statement that follows the continue statement in the loop and starts iterating from the loop entry. The continue statement is introduced in Oracle 11g version and depends on the DBMS for support.

Example of PL/SQL Continue Statement

Let's take an example of PL/SQL continue statement.

```
1. DECLARE
2.    x NUMBER := 0;
3. BEGIN
4.    LOOP - Entry point of loop
5.       DBMS_OUTPUT.PUT_LINE (Inner loop:  x = ' || TO_CHAR(x));
6.       x := x + 1;
7.       IF x < 3 THEN
8.          CONTINUE;
```

```
9.        END IF;
10.       DBMS_OUTPUT.PUT_LINE
11.         (Inner loop, after CONTINUE:  x = ' || TO_CHAR(x));
12.       EXIT WHEN x = 5;
13.     END LOOP;
14.     DBMS_OUTPUT.PUT_LINE (' After loop:  x = ' || TO_CHAR(x));
15. END;
```

After the execution of above code, you will get the following result:

```
Inner loop:  x = 0
Inner loop:  x = 1
Inner loop:  x = 2
Inner loop, after CONTINUE:  x = 3
Inner loop:  x = 3
Inner loop, after CONTINUE:  x = 4
Inner loop:  x = 4
Inner loop, after CONTINUE:  x = 5
After loop:  x = 5
```

9.7.5 GOTO Statement

The GOTO statement can take control of any specified label within the subprogram. The GOTO statement needs a label to define where to jump, and the label name can be defined between << and >>. The label name should have at least one statement following.

Syntax for GOTO

1. GOTO label_name;

Syntax for label name

1. <<label_name>>

Following points needs to be considered while using GOTO statement:

- GOTO cannot be used to transfer control into/from an IF statement, CASE statement, LOOP statement, or subblock.
- GOTO cannot transfer control from an outer block into a subblock.
- GOTO cannot transfer control out of a subprogram.
- GOTO cannot transfer control into an exception handler.

Example of PL/SQL GOTO statement   Let's take an example of PL/SQL GOTO statement.

```
1. DECLARE
2.    a number(2) := 30;
3. BEGIN
4.    <<customlabel>>
```

```
 5.     WHILE a < 41 LOOP
 6.         dbms_output.put_line ('value of a: ' || a);
 7.         a := a + 1;
 8.         IF a = 35 THEN
 9.             a := a + 1;
10.             GOTO customlabel;
11.         END IF;
12.     END LOOP;
13. END;
```

Output:

> value of a: 30
> value of a: 31
> value of a: 32
> value of a: 33
> value of a: 34
> value of a: 36
> value of a: 37
> value of a: 38
> value of a: 39
> value of a: 40
> Statement processed.

9.8 Summary

In this chapter, the basics of PL /SQL with its functions and advantages are discussed. PL/SQL is a combination of SQL along with the procedural features of programming languages. In addition, PL/SQL can be used in four different programming constructs. Conditional process control is made possible in PL/SQL using of if-then-else statements. The if statement uses a Boolean logic comparison to evaluate whether to execute the series of statements after the then clause.

Process flow can be controlled in PL/SQL with the use of loops as well. There are several different loops, from simple loop-exit statements to loop-exit when statements, while loop statements, and for loop statements. A simple loop-exit statement consists of the loop and end loop keywords enclosing the statements that will be executed repeatedly, with a special if-then statement designed to identify if an exit condition has been reached. The exit condition is identified in the while clause of the statement. Finally, the for loop statement can be used in cases where the developer wants the code repeatedly executing for a specified number of times.

References

1. Patni, J.C., Sharma, H.K., Tomar, R., & Katal, A. (2022). *Database Management System: An Evolutionary Approach* (1st ed.). Chapman and Hall/CRC. https://doi.org/10.1201/9780429282843
2. PL/SQL, 'Tutorial Points', [online]. Available: https://www.tutorialspoint.com/plsql/index.htm, [Accessed: 12 May 2022].
3. Introduction to PL/SQL, 'Oracle Tutorial', [online]. Available: https://www.oracletutorial.com/plsql-tutorial/what-is-plsql/, [Accessed: 22 May 2022].
4. 'PL/SQL Tutorials for Beginners with Examples', [online]. Available: https://www.softwaretestinghelp.com/pl-sql-tutorial/, [Accessed: 04 May 2022].
5. 'Oracle/PLSQL', [online]. Available: https://www.techonthenet.com/oracle/index.php, [Accessed: 12 February. 2022].
6. 'Introduction to PL/SQL', [online]. Available: https://oracle-base.com/articles/misc/introduction-to-plsql, [Accessed: 27 February 2022].

10

Procedures and Functions

Both stored procedures and functions are database objects which contain a set of SQL statements to complete a task. In many ways, both are different from each other. In this article, we're going to discuss the differences between stored procedures and functions.

Stored procedures are pre-compiled objects that are compiled for the first time, and their compiled format is saved, which executes (compiled code) whenever it is called.

A function is compiled and executed every time whenever it is called. A function must return a value and cannot modify the data received as parameters.

10.1 Understanding Functions

1. **IN parameters:** The IN parameters are those read-only variables that can be referenced by the procedure or function but cannot be changed.

2. **OUT parameters:** The OUT parameters are those variables that can be referenced by the procedure or function and can be changed.

3. **INOUT parameters:** The INOUT parameters are those variables that can be referenced in reading and writing mode by the procedure or function

The main and only difference between the procedures and functions is that the procedure may or may not return a value, whereas the function must return a value.

The following subsections explain the syntax with examples of procedures and functions.

10.2 Features and Advantages

- Functions in SQL have procedural language statements that support implementing the control flow logic between the traditional and dynamic SQL statements.

- Functions are easy to implement and written in high-level language that is SQL.

- The SQL functions are more reliable than other functions.

- Functions have the input and output parameters and help us to input and take the output easily.

- Functions have the return types so that we can return from the return function.

DOI: 10.1201/9781003324690-10

- We can use the multiple functions with multiple conditional statements.
- Functions are stored in the database, and we can call anytime during the execution of the program.
- We can also use recursion here in SQL functions.
- SQL functions can be invoked via the SQL triggers that we will discuss in the next section.

10.3 Types of Functions

In SQL, we generally have two types of functions are:
System-defined function: Are those functions that are already defined by the database.
User-defined: The functions that are defined by the user.

Syntax to create a function

```
1. CREATE [OR REPLACE] FUNCTION function_name [parameters]
2. [(parameter_name [IN | OUT | IN OUT] type [, ...])]
3. RETURN return_datatype
4. {IS | AS}
5. BEGIN
6.   < function_body >
7. END [function_name];
```

DROP the Function Syntax:

```
1. DROP PROCEDURE function_name;
```

Example of DROP function.

```
1. DROP PROCEDURE sumFun;
```

PL/SQL Function Example 1   This example demonstrates the function that can find the maximum of two numbers. The example consists of defining the function and calling in the same code.

```
1. DECLARE
2.   x number;
3.   y number;
4.   z number;
5. FUNCTION findMax(a IN number, b IN number)
6. RETURN number
7. IS
```

```
8.     c number;
9.  BEGIN
10.     IF a > b THEN
11.         c:= a;
12.     ELSE
13.         c:= y;
14.     END IF;
15.     RETURN c;
16. END;
17. BEGIN
18.     x:= 20;
19.     y:= 30 ;
20.
21.     z := findMax(x, y);
22.     dbms_output.put_line(' Maximum is: ' || z);
23. END;
```

Output:

Maximum is: 30

Statement processed.

PL/SQL Function Example 2
This example demonstrates the usage of SQL syntax in function and returning the result. The employee table is taken for a better understanding of the code. The function will return

TABLE 10.1

Fetching Values Using Functions

Id	Name
1	Jatin
2	Pooja
3	Shrey
4	Parisha

the total number of employees in the Table 10.1.

Function Code

```
1. CREATE OR REPLACE FUNCTION employeeCount
2. RETURN number IS
3.    result number(2) := 0;
4. BEGIN
5.    SELECT count(*) into result
```

```
6.    FROM Employee;
7.    RETURN result;
8. END;
```

After the execution of above code, you will get the following result.
Function created.

Calling the Function in PL/SQL Code

```
1. DECLARE
2.   result number(2);
3. BEGIN
4.   result := employeeCount();
5.   dbms_output.put_line('Total no. of Employee: ' || result);
6. END;
```

After the execution of the above code in SQL prompt, you will get the following result.

Total no. of Employee: 4
PL/SQL procedure successfully completed.

PL/SQL Function Example 3   This example demonstrated the recursive functions in PL/SQL to calculate the factorial of a given number. The recursive functions are the functions that call themselves. There needs to be a termination conditions to stop the recursion. In this case, the termination condition is that the factorial of 1 is always 1.

```
 1. DECLARE
 2.    ip number;
 3.    fact number;
 4. FUNCTION factorial(x number)
 5. RETURN number
 6. IS
 7.    f number;
 8. BEGIN
 9.    IF x=1 THEN
10.        f := 1;
11.    ELSE
12.        f := x * factorial(x-1);
13.    END IF;
14. RETURN f;
15. END;
16. BEGIN
17.    ip:= 5;
18.    fact := factorial(ip);
```

```
19.    dbms_output.put_line(' Factorial '|| ip || ' is ' || fact);
20. END;
```

After the execution of above code at SQL prompt, it produces the following result.

Factorial 5 is 120
PL/SQL procedure successfully completed.

10.4 Return Types

- RETURN clause specifies the data type we will return from the function.
- Function_body contains the executable part.
- The AS keyword is used instead of the IS keyword for creating a standalone function.

PL/SQL Function Example   This example demonstrates the complete process to create, call, and delete a procedure. The example creates a function to do the addition of two numbers. The code below creates a procedure, then calls it in another PL/SQL block, and finally deleting the procedure.

Function Code

```
1. create or replace function sumFun(x IN  number, y IN  number)
2. return number
3. IS
4. result number(8);
5. BEGIN
6. result :=x+y;
7. return result;
8. END;
```

Calling the Function in PL/SQL Code

```
1. DECLARE
2.  result number(2);
3. BEGIN
4.  result := sumFun(10,20);
5.  dbms_output.put_line('Addition is: ' || result);
6. END;
```

Output:

Addition is: 30
Statement processed.
0.05 seconds

10.5 Procedures

Procedures are the stored program in the database, and that can be called anytime, but the procedures don't have any return type.

Syntax for Creating Procedure

```
1. CREATE [OR REPLACE] PROCEDURE procedure_name
2.    [parameter_name TYPE DataType]
3. IS
4.    [declaration_section]
5. BEGIN
6.    executable_section
7. [EXCEPTION
8.    exception_section]
9. END [procedure_name];
```

PL/SQL Procedure Example   This example demonstrate the complete process to create, call, and delete a procedure. The example creates a procedure to insert employee in EMPLOYEE table. The code below creates an EMPLOYEE table followed by creating a procedure and then calling it in another PL/SQL block and finally deleting the procedure.

Table Creation:

```
1. create table EMPLOYEE
2. (
3. eid number(10) primary key,
4. name varchar2(100)
5. );
```

Procedure Code:

```
1. create or replace procedure "insertEmployee"
2. (eid IN NUMBER,
3. name IN VARCHAR2)
4. IS
5. BEGIN
6. insert into user values(id,name);
7. end;
```

Calling the Procedure in PL/SQL Code

```
1. BEGIN
2.    insertEmployee (101,'Jagdish');
3.    dbms_output.put_line('record inserted successfully');
4. END;
```

Now, see the "EMPLOYEE" table 10.2, you will see one record is inserted.

TABLE 10.2

Insertion via Procedure

EID	Name
101	Jagdish

DROP the Procedure Syntax:

1. DROP PROCEDURE procedure_name;

Example of drop procedure

1. DROP PROCEDURE insertEmployee;

10.6 Difference between Function and Procedure

The functions will find out the result based on the given input, and a function may return a value or control to the main program. The function divides into two parts calling program and called program. On the other hand, a procedure doesn't have the return type; it means not returning any value to the main program. Refer the table 10.3 for further differences.

TABLE 10.3

Difference Between Procedure and Functions

Parameters	Function	Procedure
Working	The functions will find out the result based on the given input.	It performs a certain task based on the input.
Exception Handling	It does not support the try-catch block.	Procedures support the try-catch block.
Calling	Can call a function in Query.	We can't call a procedure in a query.
Return	A function will have a return type.	A procedure does not support any return type.
DML Statements	We cannot use the DML statements in a function.	We can use the DML statements with procedures.
Call	We can call a function within a procedure.	Here, we cannot call a procedure within a function.

10.7 Examples

Example: Find out the sum of two numbers
Solution 1:

```
DECLARE
 i number;
 j number;
```

```
 k number;
   PROCEDURE findAdd(num1 IN number, num2 IN number, sum OUT number) IS
BEGIN
 sum := num1 + num2;
END;
BEGIN
   i:= 5;
   j:= 5;
   findAdd(i, j, k);
   dbms_output.put_line(' The sum is : ' || k);
END;
/
```

The sum is 10

Statement Processed

Solution2:

```
DECLARE
 num number;
PROCEDURE addNum(i IN OUT number) IS
BEGIN
 i := i + i;
END;
BEGIN
 num := 1;
 addNum(num);
 dbms_output.put_line('The sum is ' || num);
END;
/
```

The sum is 2

Statement Processed

Example: To find the Fibonacci series using functions.

```
create or replace function fibonacci7(n number)
return fibtype
is
fib fibtype := fibtype();
a number:=1;
b number:=1;
c number;
i number:=1;
```

```
begin
fib.extend(n);
while i<=n
 loop
    fib(i) := a;
    c:=a+b;
    a:=b;
    b:=c;
    i:=i+1;
  end loop;
return fib;
end ;
/
declare
i number;
fib fibtype := fibtype();
begin
fib := fibonacci7(6);
for i in 1..fib.count loop
 dbms_output.put_line(to_char(fib(i)));
end loop;
end;
/
```

Output:

```
1
1
2
3
5
8
```

10.8 Summary

Stored procedures are pre-compiled objects compiled for the first time and their compiled format is saved, which executes whenever it is called.

A function is compiled and executed every time whenever it is called. A function must return a value and cannot modify the data received as parameters.

Three types of parameters IN, OUT, and INOUT parameters are used to declare the functions where we can give the values and take the output with the help of these parameters. The major difference between the function and procedure is that a function has a return type and will return a value, whereas a procedure doesn't have any return type.

References

1. 'Difference Between Procedure and Functions', [online]. Available: https://www.dotnettricks. com/learn/sqlserver/difference-between-stored-procedure-and-function-in-sql-server, [Accessed: 27 January 2022].
2. 'Function Vs. Stored Procedure in SQL Server', [online]. Available: https://www.sqlshack. com/functions-vs-stored-procedures-sql-server/, [Accessed: 29 January 2022].
3. 'Determining When to Use SQL Procedures or SQL Functions', [online]. Available: https:// www.ibm.com/docs/en/db2/11.5?topic=routines-determining-when-use-sql-procedures-sql-functions, [Accessed: 22 Janaury 2022].
4. 'Procedure, Function, and Packages', [online]. Available: https://docs.oracle.com/cd/ B25329_01/doc/appdev.102/b25108/xedev_programs.htm, [Accessed: 26 January 2022].
5. 'MYSQL', [online]. Available: https://dev.mysql.com/doc/refman/8.0/en/create-procedure. html, [Accessed: 26 January 2022].
6. Patni, J.C., Sharma, H.K., Tomar, R., & Katal, A. (2022). *Database Management System: An Evolutionary Approach* (1st ed.). Chapman and Hall/CRC. https://doi.org/10.1201/9780429282843

11

Cursors and Triggers

11.1 Understanding Cursor

The part of the memory where the process statements are stored is context memory. This memory contains all intermediate results, and this can be used for the more optimized queries. To access this memory location, a cursor is used. The cursor can be resembled to pointers in some procedural language. The cursor contains the information on a select statement and the rows of data accessed by it. Further, the cursor contains attributes that can be used in PL/SQL statements.

11.2 Types of Cursors

The cursors are of two types:

1. Implicit Cursors
2. Explicit Cursors

11.2.1 Implicit Cursors

As the name states, the implicit cursors are generated automatically when an SQL statement is executed. They are generated for all DML statements. Some of the attributes that are provided by DBMS are %FOUND, %NOTFOUND, %ROWCOUNT, and %ISOPEN.

DOI: 10.1201/9781003324690-11

The following table 11.1 specifies the status of the cursor with each of its attributes.

TABLE 11.1

Types of Implicit Cursors

Attribute	Description
%FOUND	Its return value is TRUE if DML statements like INSERT, DELETE, and UPDATE affect at least one row or more rows or a SELECT INTO statement returned one or more rows. Otherwise, it returns FALSE.
%NOTFOUND	Its return value is TRUE if DML statements like INSERT, DELETE, and UPDATE affect no row, or a SELECT INTO statement return no rows. Otherwise, it returns FALSE. It is just opposite of %FOUND.
%ISOPEN	It always returns FALSE for implicit cursors because the SQL cursor is automatically closed after executing its associated SQL statements.
%ROWCOUNT	It returns the number of rows affected by DML statements like INSERT, DELETE, and UPDATE or returned by a SELECT INTO statement.

PL/SQL Implicit Cursor Example

This example demonstrates the use of SQL%ROWCOUNT attribute. The below given table is used to understand the outcome.

Create an Employee Table and Have Records

```
Create table employee
(
ID integer primary Key,
Name char(10),
Age integer,
Address varchar(20),
Salary integer
);
```

Now insert the records for the table.

```
Insert into employee values (1,  'Rakesh', 22,'Haldwani', 20000);
Insert into employee values (2,  'Hemlata', 23,'Haldwani', 22000);
Insert into employee values (3,  'Satish', 21,'Meerut', 24000);
Insert into employee values (4,  'Lokesh', 29,'Ghaziabad', 26000);
Insert into employee values (5,  'Chetan', 22,'Bulandshahr', 28000);
```

   Select* from Employee; (refer table 11.2)

TABLE 11.2

Table Employee

ID	NAME	AGE	ADDRESS	SALARY
1	Rakesh	22	Haldwani	20000
2	Hemlata	23	Haldwani	22000
3	Satish	21	Meerut	24000
4	Lokesh	29	Ghaziabad	26000
5	Chetan	22	Bulandshahr	28000

```
1.  DECLARE
2.      rows number(2);
3.  BEGIN
4.      UPDATE   Employee
5.      SET salary = salary + 5000;
6.      IF sql%notfound THEN
7.          dbms_output.put_line('no Employee updated');
8.      ELSIF sql%found THEN
9.          rows := sql%rowcount;
10.         dbms_output.put_line( rows || ' Employees updated ');
11.     END IF;
12. END;
```

Output:

5 Employees updated

PL/SQL procedure successfully completed.

Select* from employee;

Now will have the updated values of salary in the employee table 11.3

TABLE 11.3

Table Employee After Updates

ID	NAME	AGE	ADDRESS	SALARY
1	Rakesh	22	Haldwani	25,000
2	Hemlata	23	Haldwani	27,000
3	Satish	21	Meerut	29,000
4	Lokesh	29	Ghaziabad	31,000
5	Chetan	22	Bulandshahr	33,000

11.2.2 Explicit Cursors

The explicit cursor is defined in the PL/SQL block by the programmer to utilize the benefits of the context area. It is created on a SELECT statement that returns more than one row.
    Following are the typical steps using the explicit cursor:

1. Declare the cursor to initialize in the memory.
2. Open the cursor to allocate memory.
3. Fetch the cursor to retrieve data.
4. Close the cursor to release the allocated memory.

Syntax to declare a cursor

```
CURSOR name IS  SELECT statement;
```

Syntax to open a cursor

```
OPEN cursor_name;
```

```
Syntax to fetch a cursor
FETCH cursor_name INTO variable_list;
```

```
Syntax to close a cursor
Close cursor_name;
```

11.3 Examples of Cursors

PL/SQL Explicit Cursor Example

This example demonstrates the use of declaring open fetch and closing an explicit cursor. The below given table is used to understand the outcome. Observe the usage of the implicit cursor in line 11.

Refer to the above employee table:

Execute the following program to retrieve the employee's name and address.

```
DECLARE
    e_id empoyee.id%type;
    e_name employee.name%type;
    e_addr employee.address%type;
    CURSOR cursor_employee is
        SELECT id, name, address FROM employee;
BEGIN
    OPEN cursor_employee ;
    LOOP
        FETCH cursor_employee  into e_id, e_name, e_addr;
        EXIT WHEN cursor_employee %notfound;
        dbms_output.put_line(e_id || ' ' || e_name || ' ' || e_addr);
    END LOOP;
    CLOSE cursor_employee ;
END;
```

Output:

1 Rakesh Haldwani

2 Hemlata Haldwani

3 Satish Meerut

4 Lokesh Ghaziabad

5 Chetan Bulandshahr

PL/SQL procedure successfully completed.

11.4 Uses of Cursors

In SQL, a cursor is a temporary workstation allocated by the database server during the execution of a statement.

It is a database object that allows us to access data of one row at a time. This concept of SQL is useful when the user wants to update the rows of the table one by one.

The cursor in SQL is the same as the looping technique of other programming languages. The collection of tuples held by the cursor is known as the active set.

In SQL database systems, users define the cursor using the DECLARE statement and take the SELECT statement as the parameter, which helps return the set of rows.

Cursor is a database object to retrieve data from a result set one row at a time, instead of the T-SQL commands that operate on all the rows in the result set at one time. We use use-cursor-in-sql when we need to update records in a database table in a singleton fashion means row by row.

Cursor work same as looping concept. A use-cursor-in-sql is a set of rows together with a pointer that identifies a current row.

Cursors can be faster than a while loop, but have more overhead.

It is we can do RowWise validation, or in another way, you can operate on each Row. It is a data type that is used to define multivalue variables.

Cursors can be faster than a while loop but at the cost of more overhead.

It consumes more resources because use-cursor-in-sql occupies memory from the system that may be available for other processes.

Each time when a row is fetched from the use-cursor-in-sql, and it may result in a network round trip. This uses much more network bandwidth than executing a single SQL statement like SELECT or DELETE, etc., making only one round trip.

11.5 Understanding Trigger

Triggers can be understood as a scheduled procedure that happens to execute based on any event. They are configured and then automatically executed by DBMS engine without human intervention. Triggers serve many purposes, such as deriving some column values, enforcing referential integrity, event logging, auditing, replicating tables, imposing security authorizations, and preventing invalid transactions.

Triggers are executed on any of the following events and can be defined on table, view, schema, or database:

- A database operation (SERVERERROR, LOGON, LOGOFF, STARTUP, or SHUTDOWN).
- A database definition (DDL) statement (CREATE, ALTER, or DROP).
- A database manipulation (DML) statement (DELETE, INSERT, or UPDATE).

Syntax for Creating Trigger

```
CREATE [OR REPLACE ] TRIGGER trigger_name
{BEFORE | AFTER | INSTEAD OF }
{INSERT [OR] | UPDATE [OR] | DELETE}
[OF column_name]
ON table_name
[REFERENCING OLD AS o NEW AS n]
[FOR EACH ROW]
WHEN (condition)
DECLARE
 Declaration-statements
BEGIN
 Executable-statements
EXCEPTION
 Exception-handling-statements
END;
```

11.6 Types of Triggers

- CREATE [OR REPLACE] TRIGGER trigger_name: It creates or replaces an existing trigger with the trigger_name.
- {BEFORE | AFTER | INSTEAD OF}: This specifies when the trigger would be executed. The INSTEAD OF clause is used for creating trigger on a view.
- {INSERT [OR] | UPDATE [OR] | DELETE}: This specifies the DML operation.
- [OF col_name]: This specifies the column name that would be updated.
- [ON table_name]: This specifies the name of the table associated with the trigger.
- [REFERENCING OLD AS o NEW AS n]: This allows you to refer to new and old values for various DML statements like INSERT, UPDATE, and DELETE.
- [FOR EACH ROW]: This specifies a row level trigger, i.e., the trigger would be executed for each row being affected. Otherwise, the trigger will execute once when the SQL statement is executed, called a table-level trigger.
- WHEN (condition): This provides a condition for rows for which the trigger would fire. This clause is valid only for row-level triggers.

11.6.1 Row-Level Trigger

Row-level triggers are used when we have to fire the event row-wise. These events can be insert, update, or delete.

```
CREATE OR REPLACE TRIGGER trigger_name
  BEFORE | AFTER
```

```
INSERT OR DELETE OR UPDATE OF column1, column2, ...
ON table_name
FOR EACH ROW
REFERENCING OLD AS old_name
NEW AS new_name
 WHEN (condition)
   DECLARE
     ...
   BEGIN
     ...
   EXCEPTION
     ...
   END;
```

11.6.2 Table-Level Triggers

The statement-level trigger, also called table-level trigger, will be fired for every transaction, not for every row. It will fire whenever the trigger event occurs on the specified table. It will not check how many rows are impacting with statement level trigger.

The default triggers are statement-level triggers, and we are not using each row statement in statement-level trigger.

Syntax

```
CREATE OR REPLACE TRIGGER trigger_name
  BEFORE | AFTER
  INSERT OR DELETE OR UPDATE OF column1, column2, ...
  ON table_name
  REFERENCING OLD AS old_name
  NEW AS new_name
  WHEN (condition)
    DECLARE
      ...
    BEGIN
      ...
    EXCEPTION
      ...
    END;
```

11.6.3 After Trigger

After trigger will be fired after the statement is executed and will check before the insertion of the records.

Syntax

```
CREATE OR REPLACE TRIGGER trigger_name
  AFTER
  INSERT OR DELETE OR UPDATE OF column1, column2, …
  ON table_name
  REFERENCING OLD AS old_name
  NEW AS new_name
  WHEN (condition)
    DECLARE
      …
    BEGIN
      …
    EXCEPTION
      …
    END;
```

11.6.4 Before Trigger

Before trigger will be fired before the statement is executed.

Syntax

```
CREATE OR REPLACE TRIGGER trigger_name
  BEFORE
  INSERT OR DELETE OR UPDATE OF column1, column2, …
  ON table_name
  REFERENCING OLD AS old_name
  NEW AS new_name
  WHEN (condition)
    DECLARE
      …
    BEGIN
      …
    EXCEPTION
      …
    END;
```

11.7 Trigger Example

Let's take a simple example to demonstrate the trigger. In this example, we are using our same EMPLOYEE table:

Refer to the above employee table for creating the triggers.

Create Trigger

Let's take a program to create a row-level trigger for the employee table that would fire for INSERT, UPDATE, or DELETE operations performed on the employee table. This trigger will display the salary difference between the old values and new values:

```
1.  CREATE OR REPLACE TRIGGER display_salary_changes
2.  BEFORE DELETE OR INSERT OR UPDATE ON employee
3.  FOR EACH ROW
4.  WHEN (NEW.ID > 0)
5.  DECLARE
6.     sal_diff number;
7.  BEGIN
8.     sal_diff := :NEW.salary - :OLD.salary;
9.     dbms_output.put_line('Old salary: ' || :OLD.salary);
10.    dbms_output.put_line('New salary: ' || :NEW.salary);
11.    dbms_output.put_line('Salary difference: ' || sal_diff);
12. END;
```

After executing the above code at SQL Prompt, it produces the following result.

Trigger created.

Check the Salary Difference by Procedure

Use the following code to get the old salary, new salary, and salary difference after the trigger is created.

```
1.  DECLARE
2.     total_rows number(2);
3.  BEGIN
4.     UPDATE  employee
5.     SET salary = salary + 5000;
6.     IF sql%notfound THEN
7.        dbms_output.put_line('no employee updated');
8.     ELSIF sql%found THEN
9.        total_rows := sql%rowcount;
10.       dbms_output.put_line( total_rows || ' employee updated ');
11.    END IF;
12. END;
```

Output:

Old salary: 20000
New salary: 25000
Salary difference: 5000
Old salary: 22000

New salary: 27000
Salary difference: 5000
Old salary: 24000
New salary: 29000
Salary difference: 5000
Old salary: 26000
New salary: 31000
Salary difference: 5000
Old salary: 28000
New salary: 33000
Salary difference: 5000
Old salary: 30000
New salary: 35000
Salary difference: 5000
employees updated

Note: As many times we executed this code, the old and new salary is incremented by 5000, and hence, the salary difference is always 5000.

After executing the above code again, we will get the following result.

Old salary: 25000
New salary: 30000
Salary difference: 5000
Old salary: 27000
New salary: 32000
Salary difference: 5000
Old salary: 29000
New salary: 34000
Salary difference: 5000
Old salary: 31000
New salary: 36000
Salary difference: 5000
Old salary: 33000
New salary: 38000
Salary difference: 5000
Old salary: 35000
New salary: 40000
Salary difference: 5000
6 customers updated

Following are the two very important points and should be noted carefully.

- OLD and NEW references are used for record-level triggers; these are not available for table-level triggers.

If you want to query the table in the same trigger, you should use the AFTER keyword because triggers can query the table or change it again only after the initial changes are applied and the table is back in a consistent state.

11.8 Summary

A database cursor is an object that enables traversal over the rows of a result set. It allows you to process individual row returned by a query. Triggers are special PL/SQL blocks that execute when a triggering event occurs. Events that fire triggers include any SQL statement.

Using PL/SQL allows the developer to produce code that integrates seamlessly with access to the Oracle database. Examples appeared in the chapter on using all SQL statements, including data selection, data change, and transaction processing statements. No special characters or keywords are required for "embedding" SQL statements into PL/SQL because SQL is an extension of PL/SQL. As such, there really is no embedding at all. Every SQL statement executes in a cursor. When a cursor is not named, it is called an implicit cursor. PL/SQL allows the developer to investigate certain return status features in conjunction with the implicit cursors that run.

Cursor manipulation is useful when a certain operation must be performed on each row returned from a query. A cursor is simply an address in memory where a SQL statement executes. A cursor can be explicitly named with the use of the cursor cursor_name is statement, followed by the SQL statement that will comprise the cursor.

References

1. Patni, J.C., Sharma, H.K., Tomar, R., & Katal, A. (2022). *Database Management System: An Evolutionary Approach* (1st ed.). Chapman and Hall/CRC. https://doi.org/10.1201/9780429282843
2. 'PL/SQL Triggers', [online]. Available: https://www.tutorialspoint.com/plsql/plsql_triggers.htm [Accessed: 22 March 2022].
3. 'PL/SQL Cursors', [online]. Available: https://www.tutorialspoint.com/plsql/plsql_cursors.htm [Accessed: 22 March 2022].
4. PL/SQL Triggers, 'Database PL/SQL Language Reference', [online]. Available: https://docs.oracle.com/cd/E11882_01/appdev.112/e25519/triggers.htm#LNPLS020 [Accessed: 11 March 2022].
5. 'SQL Server Cursor', [online]. Available: https://www.sqlservertutorial.net/sql-server-stored-procedures/sql-server-cursor/ [Accessed: 11 May 2022].
6. 'Trigger and Cursor', [online]. Available: https://www.dotnetspider.com/forum/247141-trigger-cursor [Accessed: 11 March 2022].

12

Database Change Management

12.1 Overview

To successfully implement effective change management, it is crucial to understand a set of basic requirements. In order to ensure success, the following factors need to be incorporated into the change management discipline: intelligence, proactivity, analyses (planning and impact), automation, reliability, standardization, predictability, and quick and efficient delivery.

To manage the lifecycle of enterprise applications, an organization will need to maintain multiple replicas of an application database for various motives, such as development, production, staging, and testing. Each of these databases is designed to perform a particular process. For example, for production databases, the database needs to ensure adherence to proper production control procedures. It is important that administrators have the tools to detect unauthorized changes, such as an index being dropped without the necessary change approvals. In such scenarios, monitoring changes to production databases day over day or week over week becomes crucial.

Another important aspect of life cycle management is database compliance, ensuring that all databases meet the gold standard configuration. Abidance with organizational standards or best practices ensures that the database is efficient, maintenance is proper, and it is easy to understand.

On development databases, developers make changes that the database administrator needs to integrate and communicate to staging or test databases. The main goal is to identify the changes made to the development and then introduce the same changes to staging or test databases, taking into account any other changes already in the production database.

Most applications are going to get upgraded over time. Also, most applications are being customized by the companies to suit users' needs. Application customizations generally depend on database objects or PL/SQL modules provided by the application vendor. The application vendor supplies the scripts for upgrade, and the customer has very little clarity about the impact of the upgrade procedure on their customizations. When customers test upgrade databases, they can observe a baseline of the application schema before and after the upgrade. Comparing the before and after baselines will tell the user what modules were modified by the application. This gives them a better vision of how their customizations will be impacted as a result of upgrading their applications.

DOI: 10.1201/9781003324690-12

Three major capabilities of change management as shown in Figure 12.1 allow database administrators and developers to manage changes in database environments:

- Baseline – A point in time of defining the database and its associated database objects.
- Comparison – A complete list of differences between a baseline or a database and another baseline or a database.
- Synchronization – The process of initiating changes from a database definition captured in a baseline or from a database to a target database.

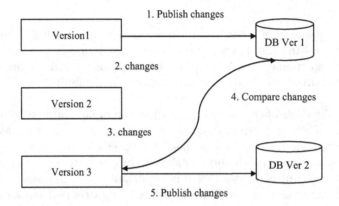

FIGURE 12.1
Change management.

As I described, we only change object's definitions. For example, we have an orders table, and in our repository, we have:

```
Create table    orders
(
Id     integer    primary Key,
Name      varchar(20)
);
Create table    orders
(
Id      integer    primary Key,
Name      varchar(30),
Description    varchar    (20)
);
```

Here, we have modified the name column and added a new attribute by description.

In the previous methods, we were executing with the help of alter command, which was a very complex process and time-consuming.

12.2 Database Definitions

A dictionary baseline includes a set of database definitions captured at a certain point in time. Baselines are stored in the Enterprise Manager repository and stored in the form of an XML document called Simple XML or SXML.

Each baseline should be assigned a unique name. A good exercise to name baselines is to match it to the scope of the database objects being captured in the baseline. A baseline can contain a series of different versions that have been captured at different points in time. By creating multiple versions of a baseline, we can track changes to the definitions of a set of database objects over time. You can simply compare two versions of the same baseline to see the changes that have occurred between them.

When creating a baseline, we also need to create a corresponding baseline scope specification, which explains the names and the types of database objects and schemas from which they must be captured. When you have developed the baseline definition, you can then capture the first version of the baseline by submitting an Enterprise Manager job. After some time, or at regular intervals, you can capture additional versions of the same baseline. Each baseline version records the metadata definitions as they occur at the time the version is captured.

12.2.1 Scope Specification

A scope specification is required in the database to identify the objects that need to be captured in a baseline. (Scope specifications also identify objects to operate in dictionary comparisons and synchronizations.) Once the scope of a baseline is specified, you cannot change the scope specification. This restriction ensure that all versions of the baseline are captured using the same set of protocols, which means that differences between versions result from changes in the database, not scope specification changes. To capture dictionary objects using a different scope specification, we need to create a new baseline.

Baseline scope specifications can take three forms.

- We can define schemas and object types to capture. For example, in schemas APPL1 and APPL2, you can capture all Tables, Indexes, and Views. When your application objects are contained in a well-defined set of schemas, this type of scope declaration is appropriate. In addition to schema objects, non-schema objects (such as Users, Roles, and Tablespaces) can also be captured and privileges granted to Users and Roles.

- Define schemas to exclude, and object types. This type of scope declaration captures objects are contained in all schemas other than those you specify. For example, in schemas other than SYSTEM and SYS, you can capture all object types. With the exception of objects contained in Oracle-provided schemas, this type of scope declaration is ideal when you want to capture all database items. You can also capture non-schema items and permission grants, just like the first type of scope specification.

- Finally, by identifying the type, schema, and name of each schema item, we may capture individual schema objects. When you want to capture a few specific objects rather than all objects contained within one or more schemas, this type of scope declaration is ideal. You can also capture non-schema items and permission grants while collecting particular schema objects.

12.2.2 Versions

Within a single dictionary baseline version, we can inspect individual object attributes, generate DDL for individual objects, and generate DDL for all the objects in the baseline version. The definitions captured in baseline versions cannot be modified since they are intended to represent the state of objects at a particular point in time.

Viewing a baseline object displays the object's properties in a graphical form.

- Choosing a baseline object and specifying "Generate DDL" shows the DDL used to create the object.
- Choosing a baseline version and specifying "Generate DDL" generates the DDL for all objects in the baseline version. While every attempt is taken to generate objects in the correct order (for example, tables come before indexes), the resulting DDL cannot always be executed on a database to produce the baseline version of the objects. For example, if you capture all of the schema objects in schema APPL1 and then try to run the baseline version DDL on a database that does not contain User APPL1, the produced DDL would fail to execute.

Baseline versions can also be used with other Change Management Pack applications, such as Compare and Synchronize. A baseline version can be compared to a database (or another baseline version). In Synchronize, we may also use a baseline version as the source of object definitions, allowing you to re-create the definitions in a different database.

Working With Multiple Dictionary Baseline Versions

When there are multiple versions of a baseline, we can examine the differences between the versions.

- Select a version and choose "View Changes Since Previous One" to examine what has changed between it and the version before it. The display shows which objects have changed, which have been added or removed, and which have remained unchanged since the previous edition. When you select an object that has changed, the differences between the two versions are displayed.
- Select a particular object and choose "View Version History" to examine how it has changed throughout all baseline versions. The display shows which versions of the object were first captured, modified, or dropped. We can compare the definitions of the object in any two baseline versions using this display.

12.2.3 Exporting/Importing Dictionaries

The export/import baseline functionality can be used for the following:

- Switching baselines between two Grid Control sites with distinct repositories.
- Offline storage of baselines. Baselines can be saved as files, erased, and then reimported.

We can select a dictionary baseline or a version, and then it can be exported to a file. For export and import, the system uses Data Pump. The Enterprise Manager Repository database server host stores the dump and log files. They can be discovered in directories set up on NFS file systems, including file systems on Oracle-supported NAS devices.

Creating Directory Objects for Export and Import

Select the directory object in the repository database for the export or import and specify a name for the export or import file to export a dictionary baseline version from the repository to an export file or import dictionary baselines from an import file on the repository database server.

To create a new directory object for export or import, the following steps are performed:

1. Log in as a user with the CREATE ANY DIRECTORY privilege or the DBA role to the repository database.

2. Assign an alias to a directory on the repository database server's file system where the baselines will be exported, or the import dump file will be kept.

3. Give SYSMAN READ and WRITE privileges to the directory object.

Enterprise Manager Administrators can pick the newly formed directory for dictionary baseline export and import. The export and import log files from the data pump are also written to the same directory.

New values for name, owner, and source database can be set during import. At the time of import, super administrators might designate another administrator as the owner.

The job information associated with a baseline is not exported by the export function. As a result, the job status will be unknown upon import.

12.3 Comparisons

A dictionary comparison detects differences in database object definitions between two baselines or databases or between two schemas within the same database/baseline.

Left and right sources, scope, and owner define a comparison specification. The scope specification specifies the names and types of database object definitions that will be compared, as well as the schemas that will contain these definitions.

Comparisons reveal differences in the values of any attribute across objects of various types. Create several variations of comparison by using comparisons. A version number and a comparison date are assigned to each version. Use these versions to connect database/schemas comparisons made over time.

Examples

Comparisons illustrate the differences between the definitions in your application's original baseline and those in your current database. It determines the differences between the original definitions at the start of the development cycle and those same definitions at the current moment after establishing a new comparison version.

To compare definitions from your most current baseline with those from your previous baseline, use a different comparison specification. The differences in the definitions from the previous baseline are identified in each newly produced version of this comparison using the comparison specification.

12.3.1 Defining Dictionary Comparisons

A dictionary comparison definition includes metadata definitions from left and right sources, scope specification, an optional schema map, and comparison options. A dictionary comparison definition cannot be changed once it has been created. This ensures that changes in the databases being compared, not the comparison's definition, are reflected in each version of the dictionary comparison.

12.3.2 Dictionary Comparison Sources

Each comparison has two sources: one on the left and one on the right. The object definitions from the left and right sources are compared. A database or a baseline version can be used as a source.

- When the source is a database, object definitions are directly pulled from the database when the comparison version is constructed.
- Object definitions are taken from the given baseline version when the source is a baseline. You can compare a database (or another baseline version) to the database as it was at a previous point in time by using a baseline version. For example, a baseline version could reflect a steady point in the application development cycle or a previous release.

There are various ways to specify the version for baseline sources.

- Specify the baseline version number if you want a certain baseline version to be used in all versions of the comparison. This is useful for comparing the database's current state to a well-defined former state, such as a release.
- You can also request that the latest or next-to-latest version can be used in the comparison. You can alternatively request that the baseline version be captured before the comparison if you provide "Latest." In one operation, you can capture a baseline and compare it to the other source. For example, you can capture a baseline version of the current state of a development database every night and compare it to the previous night's baseline or a predefined baseline reflecting a stable point in development.

12.4 Synchronizations

Differences in database object definitions between two databases or a baseline and a database are synchronized using dictionary synchronization. Database synchronization is the process of creating or modifying chosen object definitions in a database to match those in another database or a baseline.

Synchronization specifications are used to create synchronizations. The scope specification for synchronizations does not include the names of individual objects. It can only specify the kinds and schemas that should be included or excluded. You can also specify a prefix to limit the objects picked to those with names that begin with that prefix.

Differences in any attribute value between objects of any supported type are synchronized using dictionary synchronizations. To generate numerous versions of synchronization, use synchronization specifications. A version number and synchronization date are assigned to each version. Use these versions to keep track of database/schemas synchronizations over time.

12.4.1 Defining Dictionary Synchronizations

12.4.1.1 Source and Destination

The object definitions (and, optionally, data) for the destination database are provided by the synchronization source. A database or a baseline version can be used as a synchronization source. It is impossible to propagate data to the destination if the source is a baseline version, since a baseline does not capture data.

A database must always be the synchronization destination. Synchronization is the process of creating or modifying object definitions in the destination to match those in the source.

The choice for specifying which version of a source baseline to use is similar to those used with dictionary comparisons. You can use "Latest" or "Latest-1" as a fixed baseline version. You can alternatively request that the baseline version be recorded first before synchronizing the destination from it if you select "Latest."

It is critical to include all objects to be synchronized when constructing a baseline to be utilized as the source for synchronization. As a result, the baseline's scope specification should contain at least all of the synchronized schemas and object types. User and Role objects, as well as permission grants, should be included in the baseline. A baseline to database synchronization is advised in environments where updates to the source database are expected to be applied frequently, necessitating the use of a point-in-time snapshot of the database, i.e., a baseline as the synchronization source.

12.4.1.2 Synchronization Mode

The synchronization mode is the next step in defining synchronization. There are two possibilities:

- In unattended synchronization mode, the full synchronization procedure is completed in one step, ending in executing the synchronization script. If an error is identified that prevents the process from generating a valid script, the process will end without attempting to run the script.

- After the initial comparison of the source and destination items and the production of the synchronization script, interactive synchronization mode pauses. Before moving on to the next phase, you can examine the outcomes of the comparison and script generation in interactive mode and take relevant action.

12.4.2 Creating Synchronization Versions

You specify when to create the initial synchronization version after you've done specifying the synchronization. You can start working on the first version right away or later. You can also arrange for new synchronization versions to be downloaded at predetermined intervals.

The synchronization may proceed to completion (unattended mode) or pause after the initial object comparison, depending on the synchronization option you choose (interactive mode). In the latter instance, you must start a new job for each subsequent phase of the synchronization.

When using interactive mode, the destination database should not be changed between the initial comparison of the objects and the execution of the synchronization script. Otherwise, the script can have issues. Consider the case where the source contains a table that the destination does not have. The source-only table is noted in the object comparison, and the resulting script includes statements to create the table. However, you must manually construct the table at the target database after object comparison but before script execution. When the script tries to build the table, it will fail because the table already exists.

12.5 Summary

Change management in the database can help the users migrate between the different platforms and languages, making the nature of the problem easier. Versions, scope, and synchronization took place in the different types of databases. Use comparisons to create multiple versions of a comparison. Each version has a unique version number and a comparison date to easily track the versions. Use these versions to connect database/schemas comparisons. Discussed database synchronization used to create or modify selected object definitions in a database to match another database or in a baseline database.

References

1. Change Management for Databases, 'Enterprise manager Concepts', [online]. Available: https://docs.oracle.com/cd/E11857_01/em.111/e11982/change_management.htm, [Accessed: 03 May 2022].
2. Ben Rees, 'How Mature is Your Database Change Management Process?' [online]. Available: https://www.red-gate.com/simple-talk/blogs/how-mature-is-your-database-change-management-process/, [Accessed: 21 April 2022].
3. Christopher Smith, 'The Best Database Change Management Practices', [online]. Available: https://change.walkme.com/the-best-database-change-management-practices/, [Accessed: 12 April 2022].
4. Craig S. Mullins, 'Managing Database Change', *Database Trends*, October 2000.
5. Shirish Patil, (2021). 'An Effective Database Change Management System', *Database Theory and Application*, 6(1): 1–15, doi: 10.5923/j.database.20210601.0.
6. Alex Yates, http://workingwithdevs.com/rolling-back-database-changes/, 2017.
7. Chris Doig, https://www.cio.com/article/2917796/why-comparing-enterprise-software-products-with-each-other-doesnt-identify-best-fit-software.html, 2015.
8. Patni, J.C., Sharma, H.K., Tomar, R., & Katal, A. (2022). *Database Management System: An Evolutionary Approach* (1st ed.). Chapman and Hall/CRC. https://doi.org/10.1201/9780429282843

13

Sample Questions and Answers

13.1 Company Database Example

```
CREATE DATABASE ORG;
SHOW DATABASES;
USE ORG;
CREATE TABLE Worker (
    WORKER_ID INT NOT NULL PRIMARY KEY AUTO_INCREMENT,
    FIRST_NAME CHAR(25),
    LAST_NAME CHAR(25),
    SALARY INT(15),
    JOINING_DATE DATETIME,
    DEPARTMENT CHAR(25)
);

INSERT INTO Worker
    (WORKER_ID, FIRST_NAME, LAST_NAME, SALARY, JOINING_DATE, DEPARTMENT)
VALUES
        (001, 'Jagdish', 'Patni', 90000, '14-02-20', 'CSE'),
        (002, 'Priyanka', 'Sharma', 70000, '14-06-11', 'Admin'),
        (003, 'Ravi', 'Tomar', 100000, '14-02-20', 'CSE'),
        (004, 'Ajay', 'Singh', 500000, '14-02-20', 'Admin'),
        (005, 'Kapil', 'Pandey', 200000, '14-06-11', 'ECE'),
        (006, 'Anil', 'Kumar', 100000, '14-06-11', 'ECE'),
        (007, 'Satish', 'Chandra', 85000, '14-01-20', 'Account'),
        (008, 'Rakesh', 'Kumar', 90000, '14-04-11', 'Admin');
Select* from worker;
```

DOI: 10.1201/9781003324690-13

Output: shown in the table 13.1.

TABLE 13.1

Worker

WORKER_ID	FIRST_NAME	LAST_NAME	SALARY	JOINING_DATE	DEPARTMENT
001	Jagdish	Patni	90000	14-02-20	CSE
002	Priyanka	Sharma	70000	14-06-11	Admin
003	Ravi	Tomar	100000	14-02-20	CSE
004	Ajay	Singh	500000	14-02-20	Admin
005	Kapil	Pandey	200000	14-06-11	ECE
006	Anil	Kumar	100000	14-06-11	ECE
007	Satish	Chandra	85000	14-01-20	Account
008	Rakesh	Kumar	90000	14-04-11	Account

```
CREATE TABLE Bonus (
    WORKER_REF_ID INT,
    BONUS_AMOUNT INT(10),
    BONUS_DATE DATETIME,
    FOREIGN KEY (WORKER_REF_ID)
        REFERENCES Worker(WORKER_ID)
    ON DELETE CASCADE
);

INSERT INTO Bonus
    (WORKER_REF_ID, BONUS_AMOUNT, BONUS_DATE) VALUES
        (001, 5000, '16-02-20'),
        (002, 3000, '16-06-11'),
        (003, 4000, '16-02-20'),
        (001, 4500, '16-02-20'),
        (002, 3500, '16-06-11');
Select * from Bonus;
```

Output: shown in the table 13.2.

TABLE 13.2

Bonus

WORKER_REF_ID	BONUS_AMOUNT	BONUS_DATE
001	5000	16-02-20
002	3000	16-06-11
003	4000	16-02-20
001	4500	16-02-20
001	3500	16-06-11

```
CREATE TABLE Title (
    WORKER_REF_ID INT,
    WORKER_TITLE CHAR(25),
    AFFECTED_FROM DATETIME,
    FOREIGN KEY (WORKER_REF_ID)
        REFERENCES Worker(WORKER_ID)
    ON DELETE CASCADE
);

INSERT INTO Title
    (WORKER_REF_ID, WORKER_TITLE, AFFECTED_FROM) VALUES
 (001, 'Manager', '2016-02-20),
 (002, 'Executive', '2016-06-11'),
 (008, 'Executive', '2016-06-11'),
 (005, 'Manager', '2016-06-11'),
 (004, 'Asst. Manager', '2016-06-11'),
 (007, 'Executive', '2016-06-11'),
 (006, 'Lead', '2016-06-11'),
 (003, 'Lead', '2016-06-11');
Select * from title;
```

Output: shown in the table 13.3.

TABLE 13.3

Title

WORKER_REF_ID	WORKER_TITLE	AFFECTED_FROM
001	Manager	2016-02-20
002	Executive	2016-06-11
008	Executive	2016-06-11
005	Manager	2016-06-11
004	Asst. Manager	2016-06-11
007	Executive	2016-06-11
006	Lead	2016-06-11
003	Lead	2016-06-11

Once the above SQL runs, you'll see a result similar to the one attached below.

Database Created

Show Database

Use Database

Table Created

Example 1   Write an SQL query to fetch "FIRST_NAME" from the Worker table using the alias name <WORKER_NAME>.

Ans. Select FIRST_NAME AS WORKER_NAME from Worker;

Output: shown in the table 13.4.

TABLE 13.4

Example 1 Output

WORKER_NAME
Jagdish
Priyanka
Ravi
Ajay
Kapil
Anil
Satish
Rakesh

Example 2 Write an SQL query to fetch "FIRST_NAME" from the Worker table in the upper case.

Ans. Select upper(FIRST_NAME) from Worker;

Output: shown in the table 13.5.

TABLE 13.5

Example 2 Output

FIRST_NAME
JAGDISH
PRIYANKA
RAVI
AJAY
KAPIL
ANIL
SATISH
RAKESH

Example 3 Write an SQL query to fetch unique values of DEPARTMENT from the Worker table.

Ans. Select distinct DEPARTMENT from Worker;

Output: shown in the table 13.6.

TABLE 13.6

Example 3 Output

DEPARTMENT
CSE
Admin
ECE
Account

Example 4 Write an SQL query to print the first three characters of FIRST_NAME from the Worker table.

Ans. Select substring(FIRST_NAME,1,3) from Worker;

Output: shown in the table 13.7.

TABLE 13.7

Example 4 Output

FIRST_NAME
Jag
Pri
Rav
Aja
Kap
Ani
Sat
Rak

Example 5 Write an SQL query to find the position of the alphabet ('a') in the first name column 'Jagdish' from the Worker table.

Ans. Select INSTR(FIRST_NAME, BINARY'a') from Worker where FIRST_ NAME = 'Jagdish';

Output:
2

Example 6 Write an SQL query to print the FIRST_NAME from the Worker table after removing white spaces from the right side.

Ans. Select RTRIM(FIRST_NAME) from Worker;

Example 7 Write an SQL query to print the DEPARTMENT from the Worker table after removing white spaces from the left side.

Ans. Select LTRIM(DEPARTMENT) from Worker;

Example 8 Write an SQL query that fetches the unique values of DEPARTMENT from the Worker table and prints its length.

Ans. Select distinct length(DEPARTMENT) from Worker;

Example 9 Write an SQL query to print the FIRST_NAME from the Worker table after replacing 'a' with 'A'.

Ans. Select REPLACE(FIRST_NAME,'a','A') from Worker;

Example 10 Write an SQL query to print the FIRST_NAME and LAST_NAME from the Worker table into a single column COMPLETE_NAME. A space char should separate them.

Ans. Select CONCAT(FIRST_NAME, ' ', LAST_NAME) AS 'COMPLETE_NAME' from Worker;

Output: shown in the table 13.8.

TABLE 13.8

Example 10 Output

COMPLETE_NAME
Jagdish Patni
Priyanka Sharma
Ravi Tomar
Ajay Sharma
Kapil Pandey
Anil Kumar
Satish Chandra
Rakesh Kumar

Example 11   Write an SQL query to print all the Worker details from the Worker table order by FIRST_NAME Ascending.

Ans. Select * from Worker order by FIRST_NAME asc;

Output: shown in the table 13.9.

TABLE 13.9

Example 11 Output

WORKER_ID	FIRST_NAME	LAST_NAME	SALARY	JOINING_DATE	DEPARTMENT
004	Ajay	Singh	500000	14-02-20	Admin
006	Anil	Kumar	100000	14-06-11	ECE
001	Jagdish	Patni	90000	14-02-20	CSE
005	Kapil	Pandey	200000	14-06-11	ECE
002	Priyanka	Sharma	70000	14-06-11	Admin
008	Rakesh	Kumar	90000	14-04-11	Account
003	Ravi	Tomar	100000	14-02-20	CSE
007	Satish	Chandra	85000	14-01-20	Account

Example 12   Write an SQL query to print all the Worker details from the Worker table order by FIRST_NAME Ascending and DEPARTMENT Descending.

Ans. Select * from Worker order by FIRST_NAME asc,DEPARTMENT desc;

Example 13   Write an SQL query to print details for the Workers with the first name "Ajay" and "Satish" from the Worker table.

Ans. Select * from Worker where FIRST_NAME in ('Ajay','Satish');

Example 14   Write an SQL query to print details of workers excluding first names, "Ajay" and "Satish" from the Worker table.

Ans. Select * from Worker where FIRST_NAME not in ('Ajay','Satish');

Example 15   Write an SQL query to print details of the Workers with DEPARTMENT name "Admin".

Ans. Select * from Worker where DEPARTMENT like 'Admin%';

TABLE 13.10

Example 15 Output shown in the table 13.10

WORKER_ID	FIRST_NAME	LAST_NAME	SALARY	JOINING_DATE	DEPARTMENT
002	Priyanka	Sharma	70000	14-06-11	Admin
004	Ajay	Singh	500000	14-02-20	Admin

Example 16   Write an SQL query to print details of the Workers whose FIRST_NAME contains 'a'.

Ans. Select * from Worker where FIRST_NAME like '%a%';
Output: shown in the table 13.11.

TABLE 13.11

Example 16 Output

WORKER_ID	FIRST_NAME	LAST_NAME	SALARY	JOINING_DATE	DEPARTMENT
001	Jagdish	Patni	90000	14-02-20	CSE
002	Priyanka	Sharma	70000	14-06-11	Admin
003	Ravi	Tomar	100000	14-02-20	CSE
004	Ajay	Singh	500000	14-02-20	Admin
005	Kapil	Pandey	200000	14-06-11	ECE
007	Satish	Chandra	85000	14-01-20	Account
008	Rakesh	Kumar	90000	14-04-11	Account

Example 17   Write an SQL query to print details of the Workers whose FIRST_NAME ends with 'a'.

Ans. Select * from Worker where FIRST_NAME like '%a';
Output: shown in the table 13.12.

TABLE 13.12

Example 17 Output

WORKER_ID	FIRST_NAME	LAST_NAME	SALARY	JOINING_DATE	DEPARTMENT
002	Priyanka	Sharma	70000	14-06-11	Admin

Example 18   Write an SQL query to print details of the Workers whose FIRST_NAME ends with 'h' and contains six alphabets.

Ans. Select * from Worker where FIRST_NAME like '_____h';
Output: shown in the table 13.13.

TABLE 13.13

Example 18 Output

WORKER_ID	FIRST_NAME	LAST_NAME	SALARY	JOINING_DATE	DEPARTMENT
007	Satish	Chandra	85000	14-01-20	Account

Example 19   Write an SQL query to print details of the Workers whose SALARY lies between 100,000 and 500,000.

Ans. Select * from Worker where SALARY between 100000 and 500000;

Output: shown in the table 13.14.

TABLE 13.14

Example 19 Output

WORKER_ID	FIRST_NAME	LAST_NAME	SALARY	JOINING_DATE	DEPARTMENT
003	Ravi	Tomar	100000	14-02-20	CSE
004	Ajay	Singh	500000	14-02-20	Admin
005	Kapil	Pandey	200000	14-06-11	ECE
006	Anil	Kumar	100000	14-06-11	ECE

Example 20   Write an SQL query to print details of the Workers who joined in Feb'2020.

Ans. Select * from Worker where year(JOINING_DATE) = 2020 and month(JOINING_DATE) = 2;

Output: shown in the table 13.15.

TABLE 13.15

Example 20 Output

WORKER_ID	FIRST_NAME	LAST_NAME	SALARY	JOINING_DATE	DEPARTMENT
001	Jagdish	Patni	90000	14-02-20	CSE
003	Ravi	Tomar	100000	14-02-20	CSE
004	Ajay	Singh	500000	14-02-20	Admin

Example 21   Write an SQL query to fetch the count of employees working in the department 'Admin'.

Ans. SELECT COUNT(*) FROM worker WHERE DEPARTMENT = 'Admin';

Output:

2

Example 22   Write an SQL query to fetch the worker names with salaries >= 50,000 and <= 100,000.

Ans. SELECT CONCAT(FIRST_NAME, ' ', LAST_NAME) As Worker_Name, Salary FROM worker WHERE WORKER_ID IN (SELECT WORKER_ID FROM worker WHERE Salary BETWEEN 50000 AND 100000);

Output: shown in the table 13.16.

TABLE 13.16
Example 22 Output

Worker_Name	SALARY
Jagdish Patni	90000
Priyanka Sharma	70000
Satish Chandra	85000
Rakesh Kumar	90000

Example 23   Write an SQL query to fetch the number of workers for each department in descending order.

Ans. SELECT DEPARTMENT, count(WORKER_ID) No_Of_Workers

FROM worker GROUP BY DEPARTMENT ORDER BY No_Of_Workers DESC;

Output: shown in the table 13.17.

TABLE 13.17
Example 23 Output

DEPARTMENT	No_Of_Workers
CSE	02
Admin	02
ECE	02
Account	02

Example 24   Write an SQL query to print details of the Workers who are also Managers.

Ans. SELECT DISTINCT W.FIRST_NAME, T.WORKER_TITLE FROM Worker W INNER JOIN Title T ON W.WORKER_ID = T.WORKER_REF_ID AND T.WORKER_TITLE in ('Manager');

Output: shown in the table 13.18.

TABLE 13.18
Example 24 Output

FIRST_NAME	WORKER_TITLE
Jagdish	Manager
Kapil	Nanager

Example 25   Write an SQL query to fetch duplicate records having matching data in some fields of a table.

Ans. SELECT WORKER_TITLE, AFFECTED_FROM, COUNT(*) FROM Title GROUP BY WORKER_TITLE, AFFECTED_FROM HAVING COUNT(*) > 1;

Example 26   Write an SQL query to show only odd rows from a table.

Ans. SELECT * FROM Worker WHERE MOD (WORKER_ID, 2) <> 0;

Output: shown in the table 13.19.

TABLE 13.19

Example 26 Output

WORKER_ID	FIRST_NAME	LAST_NAME	SALARY	JOINING_DATE	DEPARTMENT
001	Jagdish	Patni	90000	14-02-20	CSE
003	Ravi	Tomar	100000	14-02-20	CSE
005	Kapil	Pandey	200000	14-06-11	ECE
007	Satish	Chandra	85000	14-01-20	Account

Example 27   Write an SQL query to show only even rows from a table.

Ans. SELECT * FROM Worker WHERE MOD (WORKER_ID, 2) = 0;

Output: shown in the table 13.20.

TABLE 13.20

Example 27 Output

WORKER_ID	FIRST_NAME	LAST_NAME	SALARY	JOINING_DATE	DEPARTMENT
002	Priyanka	Sharma	70000	14-06-11	Admin
004	Ajay	Singh	500000	14-02-20	Admin
006	Anil	Kumar	100000	14-06-11	ECE
008	Rakesh	Kumar	90000	14-04-11	Account

Example 28   Write an SQL query to clone a new table from another table.

Ans. SELECT * INTO WorkerClone FROM Worker;

Example 29   Write an SQL query to fetch intersecting records of two tables.

Ans. (SELECT * FROM Worker) INTERSECT (SELECT * FROM WorkerClone);

Example 30   Write an SQL query to show records from one table that another table does not have.

Ans. SELECT * FROM Worker MINUS SELECT * FROM Title;

Example 31   Write an SQL query to show the current date and time.

Ans. SELECT getdate();

Example 32 Write an SQL query to show a top n (say 10) records of a table.

Ans. SELECT TOP 10 * FROM Worker ORDER BY Salary DESC;

Example 33 Write an SQL query to determine the nth (say n=5) highest salary from a table.

Ans. SELECT TOP 1 Salary FROM (SELECT DISTINCT TOP n Salary

FROM Worker ORDER BY Salary DESC) ORDER BY Salary ASC;

Example 34 Write an SQL query to determine the fifth highest salary without using TOP or limit method.

Ans. SELECT Salary FROM Worker W1

WHERE 4 = (SELECT COUNT(DISTINCT (W2.Salary)) FROM Worker W2

WHERE W2.Salary >= W1.Salary);

Example 35 Write an SQL query to fetch the list of employees with the same salary.

Ans. Select distinct W.WORKER_ID, W.FIRST_NAME, W.Salary from Worker W, Worker W1 where W.Salary = W1.Salary and W.WORKER_ID != W1.WORKER_ID;

Example 36 Write an SQL query to show the second highest salary from a table.

Ans. Select max(Salary) from Worker where Salary not in (Select max(Salary) from Worker);

Example 37 Write an SQL query to show one row twice in results from a table.

Ans. select FIRST_NAME, DEPARTMENT from worker W where W.DEPARTMENT='Admin' union all select FIRST_NAME, DEPARTMENT from Worker W1 where W1.DEPARTMENT='Admin';

Example 38 Write an SQL query to fetch intersecting records of two tables.

Ans. (SELECT * FROM Worker) INTERSECT (SELECT * FROM WorkerClone);

Example 39 Write an SQL query to fetch the first 50% of records from a table.

Ans. SELECT *FROM WORKER WHERE WORKER_ID <= (SELECT count(WORKER_ID)/2 from Worker);

Example 40 Write an SQL query to fetch the departments with less than five people.

Ans. SELECT DEPARTMENT, COUNT(WORKER_ID) as 'Number of Workers' FROM Worker GROUP BY DEPARTMENT HAVING COUNT(WORKER_ID) < 5;

Example 41 Write an SQL query to show all departments along with the number of people there.

Ans. SELECT DEPARTMENT, COUNT(DEPARTMENT) as 'Number of Workers' FROM Worker GROUP BY DEPARTMENT;

Example 42 Write an SQL query to show the last record from a table.

Ans. Select * from Worker where WORKER_ID = (SELECT max(WORKER_ID) from Worker);

Example 43   Write an SQL query to fetch the first row of a table.

Ans. Select * from Worker where WORKER_ID = (SELECT min(WORKER_ID) from Worker);

Example 44   Write an SQL query to fetch the last five records from a table.

Ans. SELECT * FROM Worker WHERE WORKER_ID <=5 UNION SELECT * FROM (SELECT * FROM Worker W order by W.WORKER_ID DESC) AS W1 WHERE W1.WORKER_ID <=5;

Example 45   Write an SQL query to print the name of employees having the highest salary in each department.

Ans. SELECT t.DEPARTMENT,t.FIRST_NAME,t.Salary from(SELECT max(Salary) as TotalSalary,DEPARTMENT from Worker group by DEPARTMENT) as TempNew Inner Join Worker t on TempNew.DEPARTMENT=t.DEPARTMENT and TempNew.TotalSalary=t.Salary;

Example 46   Write an SQL query to fetch three max salaries from a table.

Ans. SELECT distinct Salary from worker a WHERE 3 >= (SELECT count(distinct Salary) from worker b WHERE a.Salary <= b.Salary) order by a.Salary desc;

Example 47   Write an SQL query to fetch three min salaries from a table.

Ans. SELECT distinct Salary from worker a WHERE 3 >= (SELECT count(distinct Salary) from worker b WHERE a.Salary >= b.Salary) order by a.Salary desc;

Example 48   Write an SQL query to fetch nth max salaries from a table.

Ans. SELECT distinct Salary from worker a WHERE n >= (SELECT count(distinct Salary) from worker b WHERE a.Salary <= b.Salary) order by a.Salary desc;

Example 49   Write an SQL query to fetch departments along with the total salaries paid for each of them.

Ans. SELECT DEPARTMENT, sum(Salary) from worker group by DEPARTMENT;

Example 50   Write an SQL query to fetch the names of workers who earn the highest salary.

Ans. SELECT FIRST_NAME, SALARY from Worker WHERE SALARY=(SELECT max(SALARY) from Worker);

13.2 Fill in the Blanks

1. A .... is a collection of objects you need to store and manipulate data, such as table.

2 A .... key is a column or a set of columns that uniquely identifies each row in the table.

3. .... are some rules that help ensure the validity of the data while entering it into a table.

4. The .... TABLE command is used to modify the table structure.

5. To select a specific row(s), ... clause is used in the query.
6. The .... clause compares one string value with another.

Answers:
1. Database
2. Primary
3. Constraints
4. Alter
5. Where
6. Like

13.3 True and False

1. The SHOW DATABASES; query will display all the tables.
2. The USE command is used to activate a database.
3. The query DESC student; will display information on the fields in the table 'student'.
4. To display only unique values, the DISTINCT clause is used.
5. The two wildcard characters used with the LIKE clause are * and ?.

Answers:
1. False
2. True
3. False
4. True
5. False

13.4 Multiple Choice Questions

1. SQL is a(n) _____ database management system ?
   a. Object oriented
   b. Hierarchical
   c. Relational
   d. Network
2. What is the data in a MySQL database??
   a. Objects
   b. Tables
   c. Networks
   d. File systems

3. How is the communication established with MySQL server?
    a. SQL
    b. Network calls
    c. A programming language like C++
    d. APIs

4. What is a tuple in a relational database?
    a. Table
    b. Row
    c. Column
    d. Object

5. What represents an attribute in a relational database?
    a. Table
    b. Row
    c. Column
    d. Object

6. Which statement is used to select a database?
    a. USE
    b. CREATE
    c. DROP
    d. SCHEMA

7. What keyword is the synonym for DATABASE?
    a. TABLE
    b. OBJECT
    c. DB
    d. SCHEMA

8. What keyword is used to create a database?
    a. CREATE
    b. SET
    c. SETUP
    d. LINK

9. The file created by the server to store the database attributes is _____?
    a. db.otp
    b. dp.zip
    c. db.opt
    d. db.cls

10. Which statement does not use the same number of bytes, and the byte usage depends on the input data?
    a. Varchar
    b. Char
    c. Both Varchar and Char
    d. None of the above

11. The maximum length of a column of type "char" is _____?
    a. 255 bytes
    b. 65, 535 bytes
    c. 256 bytes
    d. None of the above

12. To create a database only if it does not already exist, which clause is used?
    a. IF EXISTS
    b. IF NOT EXISTS
    c. CREATE EXISTS
    d. EXISTS IF

13. Is it possible to write COLLATE expression without CHARACTER SET?
    a. True
    b. False

14. What does "salary" represent in the following query?

    ```
    CREATE TABLE emp
    (
    id number not null,
    salary number(9,3),
    hiring_date DATE,
    birth_date DATE
    )
    ```

    a. Table
    b. Row
    c. Column
    d. Object

15. Which MySQL instance is responsible for processing the data?
    a. MySQL client
    b. MySQL server
    c. SQL
    d. Daemon program

16. What statement is used to show the definition of an existing database?
    a. Show Database
    b. Create Database
    c. Use Database
    d. Create Table

17. In SQL databases, the structure representing the organizational views of all databases is _____ ?
    a. Schema
    b. View
    c. Instance
    d. Table

18. Which of the following statements arecorrect for choosing the non-default character set?

    a. Varchar (20) Character set utf8;

    b. Varchar(20);

    c. Varchar(20) character set;

    d. None

19. Which of the following TEXT type has the maximum number of bytes?

    a. Tiny text

    b. Text

    c. Medium text

    d. Long text

20. Which of the following has the maximum number of bytes?

    a. Varchar

    b. Char

    c. Text

    d. Both Varchar and Char

21. Which statement makes changes to database attributes?

    a. CHANGE

    b. ALTER

    c. ALTERNATE

    d. UPDATE

22. What happens if the data stored in a column of type Text exceeds the maximum size of that type?

    a. Extra memory will be allocated

    b. End the process

    c. Data will be truncated

    d. Depends on the system

23. Which data type is best suited for storing "small texts" in MySQL?

    a. Char

    b. Varchar

    c. Mediumtext

    d. Longtext

24. Which data type is best suited for storing "documents" in MySQL?

    a. Char

    b. Varchar

    c. Mediumtext

    d. Longtext

25. Numeric types are used to describe _____?

    a. Integers numbers

    b. Natural numbers

    c. Rational numbers

    d. Integers and natural numbers

26. Which numeric type has the largest range?

    a. Mediumint

    b. Smallint

    c. Int

    d. Tinyint

27. What will be the storage form for "float(4,2)" in MySQL?

    a. Total of four digits, two to the left and two to the right of the decimal

    b. Total of six digits

    c. Total of four digits, not evenly distributed

    d. None of the above

28. What is the default format for the data type "Date"?

    a. YYYY-MM-DD

    b. MM-YYYY-DD

    c. DD-MM-YYYY

    d. None of the above

29. The place where the server stores its databases and status files are called "data"?

    a. True

    b. False

30. The maximum value for FLOAT is _____?

    a. 3.402823466E+38

    b. 3.402823466E+37

    c. 3.402823466E+39

    d. 3.402823466E+35

31. Which of the following value displays an error when stored in "float(4,2)"?

    a. 12.11

    b. 13.1

    c. 1.12

    d. 123.44

32. Are "Datetime" and "Timestamp" the same data type?

    a. Yes

    b. No

    c. Depends on DBMS

    d. None of the above

33. What is the default format for the data type "Time"?

    a. HHH:MI:SS

    b. SS:MI:HHH

    c. MI:SS:HHH

    d. None of the above

34. What is the default format for the data type "Year"?
    a. YYYY
    b. YYYY-DD-MM
    c. MM-YYYY-DD
    d. None of the above

35. Which of the following is the correct representation of "float(5,0)"?
    a. 12345.123
    b. 12345.1
    c. 12345
    d. 123.123

36. Which of the following is the correct representation of "float(4,2)"?
    a. 24,33
    b. 124,4
    c. 12.123
    d. 24.33 et 124

37. The size of the BIT type is _____ ?
    a. 1
    b. 2
    c. 3
    d. Variable

38. Which of the following command is used to drop an existing table?
    a. DROP TABLE
    b. DELETE
    c. Both A and B
    d. None of the above

39. Which of the following command is used to display all existing tables in a database?
    a. SHOW TABLES
    b. SHOW TABLE
    c. SHOW
    d. None of the above

40. Is duplicate primary key allowed in SQL?
    a. Yes
    b. No
    c. Depends on DBMS
    d. None of the above

41. Is duplication of attributes allowed in SQL?
    a. Yes
    b. No

    c. Depends on DBMS

    d. None of the above

42. What is the correct format for storing the date in SQL?

    a. DEC-01-1994

    b. 08-1994-12

    c. 08-DEC-16

    d. 1994-12-08

43. Which of following the following statement will produce an error?

    a. Select * from emp where empid=1;

    b. Select empname from emp;

    c. Select salary from emp;

    d. None of the above

44. What key is used to link two tables in MySQL?

    a. Primary key

    b. Foreign key

    c. Primary and foreign key

    d. None of the above

45. Find the error?

```
CREATE TABLE person (
person_id SMALLINT,
lastname VARCHAR,
FIRSTNAME VARCHAR,
birth_date DATE
CONSTRAINTS pk_person PRIMARY KEY (person_id)
);
INSERT INTO
personne( person_id, lastname, FIRSTNAME, Birth_date )
VALUES(1,'a','b', 09-1994-02);
```

    a. Error in data values

    b. No Error

    c. Other error

    d. None of the above

46. Find the error?

```
CREATE TABLE person (
person_id SMALLINT,
lastname VARCHAR,
FIRSTNAME VARCHAR,
birth_date DATE
CONSTRAINTS pk_person PRIMARY KEY (person_id)
);
```

```
INSERT INTO
person( person_id, lastname, FIRSTNAME)
VALUES(1, 'a', 'b');
INSERT INTO
person( person_id, lastname, FIRSTNAME)
VALUES(1,'c','d');
```

    a. No Error

    b. Error, duplicate value

    c. Other error

    d. None of the above

47. What are the valid data types in MySQL?

    a. Numeric

    b. Temporary

    c. Text

    d. All the answers are true

48. Which clause determines which column to include in the query sets?

    a. SELECT

    b. FROM

    c. WHERE

    d. ORDER BY

49. Which clause is used to identify the table?

    a. SELECT

    b. FROM

    c. WHERE

    d. ORDER BY

50. Which clause is used to filter the data?

    a. SELECT

    b. FROM

    c. WHERE

    d. ORDER BY

51. Which clause is used to group rows by common column values?

    a. SELECT

    b. GROUP BY

    c. ORDER BY

    d. WHERE

52. Which clause is used to filter groups?

    a. HAVING

    b. FROM

    c. WHERE

    d. SELECT

53. Which clause is used to sort the result by one or more columns?

    a. HAVING

    b. FROM

    c. ORDER BY

    d. WHERE

54. The keyword "MODIFY" is used with which query clause?

    a. ALTER

    b. FROM

    c. WHERE

    d. ORDER BY

55. Which of the following is not a query clause?

    a. WHERE

    b. MODIFY

    c. ALTER

    d. FROM

56. Which clause is used to modify the existing field of the table?

    a. ALTER

    b. FROM

    c. SELECT

    d. MODIFY

57. What statement is used to show the definition of an existing database?

    a. SHOW CREATE DATABASE

    b. SHOW DATABASE

    c. SHOW CREATE

    d. SHOW CREATE DATABASE TABLE

Answers:

    1. C

    2. B

    3. A

    4. B

    5. C

    6. A

    7. D

    8. A

    9. C

   10. A

11. A
12. B
13. A
14. C
15. B
16. A
17. A
18. A
19. D
20. C
21. B
22. C
23. C
24. D
25. D
26. C
27. A
28. A
29. A
30. A
31. D
32. D
33. A
34. A
35. C
36. D
37. D
38. A
39. A
40. B
41. A
42. D
43. D
44. B
45. A
46. B
47. D
48. A
49. B

50. C
51. B
52. A
53. C
54. A
55. B
56. A
57. A

Index

A

ADD (+), 95
aggregate function, 64
    Avg(), 64
    Count(), 66
    Max(), 68
    Min(), 67
    Sum(), 67
alternate key, 48
arithmetic operators, 84
assembly language, 77
attributes, 9
authentication, 23
auto increment sequence, 139
automation, 183

B

backup, 3
baseline, 184
    dictionary baseline, 185
    export/import, 186
    scope specification, 185
    versions, 186
bit operators, 84

C

Cache, 8
Call, 167
candidate key, 48
cardinality, 12
case statement, 157
change management, 190
Character Functions, 86
check constraints, 53, 79
cloud databases, 5
comments, 145
comparison, 187
    dictionary comparison, 187
comparison operators, 84, 100
    equal to (=), 100
    greater than (), 100
    greater than equal to (=), 100

less than (), 100
    less than equal to (=), 100
compound key, 48
conditional statements, 89
    CASE Statement, 90
    IF statement, 90
    For statement, 92
    While statement, 91
constants, 145
constraints, 78
CREATE, 19
cursors, 171
    explicit cursor, 173
    implicit cursor, 171
cycle, 139

D

database management system, 1
Database Manager, 7
data control language (DCL), 16, 34
data definition language (DDL), 15, 27
    Alter, 27
    Create, 27
    Drop, 27
    Rename, 27
    Truncate, 27
data dictionary, 37
data integrity, 45
    domain integrity, 45
    entity integrity, 46
    referential integrity, 47
    user-defined integrity, 47
data manager, 37
data manipulation language (DML), 15, 31
    Delete, 15, 31
    Insert into, 31
    Select, 31
    Update, 31
data sharing, 3
data types, 20, 78
data warehouses, 4
date and time, 22
Date Functions, 86

DDL compiler, 37
delimiters, 145
design issues, 78
distinct, 62
distributed databases, 4
DIVISION (/), 95
DML statements, 167
domain constraints, 55

E

efficient delivery, 183
Enterprise Manager, 185
entity, 9
entity integrity constraints, 78
entity relationship (ER) model, 8
error checking, 145
Exception Handling, 167
EXECUTE, 16

F

fixed-length, 83
foreign key, 13, 48
for loop, 151
FOUND, 179
function based indexes, 138
functions, 161

G

graph databases, 4
GROUP BY, 71

H

HAVING, 72
hierarchical databases, 6
high-level programming languages, 78

I

identifiers, 145
if-else, 149
indexes, 135
    reverse index, 136
    unique index, 137
IN-OUT parameter, 162
IN parameter, 162
INSERT, 16
intelligence, 183

J

join, 118
    EQUI JOIN, 119
    INNER JOIN, 118
    left OUTER JOIN, 121
    OUTER JOIN, 118
    right OUTER JOIN, 124
JSON database, 5

L

literals, 145
Log Devices, 85
logical operator, 104
    AND, 106
    Between, 107
    IN, 108
    ANY, 104
    NOT, 110
    OR, 106

M

Mathematical Functions, 86
MODULUS (%), 95
multimodel database, 5
MULTIPLY (*), 95
MySQL, 17

N

nested query, 115
network databases, 7
No cycle, 139
nonprocedural language, 17
NoSQL databases, 4
NOTFOUND, 179

O

object-oriented databases, 4
OLTP databases, 4
open source databases, 5
Order By, 68
OUT parameter, 161

P

planning and impact, 183
PL/SQL, 145
    data types, 146

predicate, 63
predictability, 183
primary key, 13, 48
proactivity, 183
procedures, 161

Q

query optimizer, 37

R

recovery manager, 77
redundancy, 14
referential integrity constraints, 79
relational databases, 4
relationship, 9
reliability, 183
Return, 165

S

schema object names, 78
segments, 85
SELECT, 19
self-driving databases, 5
sequences, 79, 139
set operators, 84
SQL, 17
    Server, 10
standardization, 183
stored procedures, 78
string operators, 84
structured query language (SQL), 17
subquery, 115
super key, 48
surrogate key, 48

SUSTRACT (-), 95
synchronization, 188

T

tablespace, 85
transaction control language (TCL), 16, 35
    AUTOCOMMIT, 36
    COMMIT, 35
    ROLLBACK, 35
    SAVEPOINT, 36
triggers, 78, 175
    after trigger, 177
    row level trigger, 176
    statement level trigger, 177
    before trigger, 179

U

UNIQUE constraints, 54
unique key constraints, 79
UPDATE, 15
user defined, 162
users, 78

V

varying-length, 83
VIEW, 129
views, 78
    composite view, 130, 132
    simple view, 130

W

when, 150
while statement, 153

Printed in the United States
by Baker & Taylor Publisher Services